The WAC Journal

Writing Across the Curriculum
Volume 30
2019

© 2019 Clemson University
Printed on acid-free paper in the USA
ISSN: 1544-4929

Editors

Cameron Bushnell, Clemson University
David Blakesley, Clemson University

Managing Editor

Stacy Cacciatore, Clemson University

Editorial Board

Heather Bastian, UNC Charlotte
Jacob S. Blumner, University of Michigan, Flint
Heather Falconer, Curry College
Michael LeMahieu, Clemson University
Carol Rutz, Carleton College
Terry Myers Zawacki, George Mason University

Copyeditor

Jared Jameson

Review board

Will Banks, East Carolina University
Kristine Blair, Duquesne University
Rasha Diab, University of Texas at Austin

Patricia Donahue, Lafayette College
John Eliason, Gonzaga University
Jeff Galin, Florida Atlantic University
Melissa Goldwaithe, Saint Joseph's University
Bradley Hughes, University of Wisconsin
Anna Knutson, Duquesne University
Michelle LaFrance, George Mason University
Christina LaVecchia, Neumann Univ and Mayo Clinic
Sean Morey, University of Tennessee, Knoxville
Lee Nickoson, Bowling Green State University
Sarah Peterson Pittock, Stanford University
Rebecca Pope-Ruark, Elon University
Jenna Pack Sheffield, University of New Haven
Douglas Walls, North Carolina State University
Xiqiao Wang, Michigan State University
Carrie Wastal, University of California, San Diego
Joanna Wolfe, Carnegie Mellon University
David Zehr, Plymouth State University

Subscription Information

The WAC Journal
Parlor Press
3015 Brackenberry Drive
Anderson SC 29621
wacjournal@parlorpress.com
parlorpress.com/wacjournal
Rates: 1 year: $25; 3 years: $65; 5 years: $95.

Submissions

The editorial board of *The WAC Journal* seeks WAC-related articles from across the country. Our national review board welcomes inquiries, proposals, and 3,000 to 6,000 word articles on WAC-related topics, including the following: WAC Techniques and Applications; WAC Program Strategies; WAC and WID; WAC and Writing Centers; Interviews and Reviews. Proposals and articles outside these categories will also be considered. Any discipline-standard documentation style (MLA, APA, etc.) is acceptable, but please follow such guidelines carefully. Submissions are managed initially via Submittable (https://parlorpress.submittable.com/submit) and then via email. For general inquiries, contact Lea Anna Cardwell, the managing editor, via email (wacjournal@parlorpress.com). The WAC Journal is an open-access, blind, peer-viewed journal published annually by Clemson University, Parlor Press, and the WAC Clearinghouse. It is available in print through Parlor Press and online in open-access format at the WAC Clearinghouse. *The WAC Journal* is peer-reviewed. It is published annually by Clemson University, Parlor Press, and the WAC Clearinghouse.

Subscriptions

The WAC Journal is published annually in print by Parlor Press and Clemson University. Digital copies of the journal are simultaneously published at The WAC Clearinghouse in PDF format for free download. Print subscriptions support the ongoing publication of the journal and make it possible to offer digital copies as open access. Subscription rates: One year: $25; Three years: $65; Five years: $95. You can subscribe to The WAC Journal and pay securely by credit card or PayPal at the Parlor

Press website: http://www.parlorpress.com/wacjournal. Or you can send your name, email address, and mailing address along with a check (payable to Parlor Press) to Parlor Press, 3015 Brackenberry Drive, Anderson SC 29621. Email: sales@parlorpress.com

Reproduction of material from this publication, with acknowledgement of the source, is hereby authorized for educational use in non-profit organizations.

The WAC Journal
Volume 30, 2019

Contents

ARTICLES

Reading an Institution's History of WAC through
the Lens of Whole-Systems Theory 7
BRAD PETERS

Designing for "More": Writing's Knowledge and
Epistemologically Inclusive Teaching 35
LINDA ADLER-KASSNER

Threading Competencies in Writing Courses for More Effective Transfer 64
AMY D. WILLIAMS AND JONATHAN BALZOTTI

The Material Contexts of Writing Assignment Design 86
THOMAS POLK

REVIEW 108

    Dannels, Deanna P., Patricia R. Palmerton, and Amy L. H. Gaffney. *Oral Communication in the Disciplines: A Resource for Teacher Development and Training*

REVIEWED BY AMY CICCHINO

Contributors 115

Reading an Institution's History of WAC through the Lens of Whole-Systems Theory

BRAD PETERS

This case study of a WAC program at a high-research university uses a whole-systems approach to long-term programmatic evaluation. The study underscores the role that a university writing center can play in providing meaningful data for analyzing the historical ebb and flow of WAC in the presence and absence of supports necessary to sustain WAC's momentum. The study suggests how to develop a rubric for measuring and interpreting such data at important historical checkpoints, to assemble a story that can inform a university about how past challenges and successes will help a WAC program move toward integration with key elements of a university's social, economic, and institutional systems. As such, this modeled reading of WAC's history at one university promises to inform WAC leadership at other universities about how they might gather and interpret evidence that paves the way for WAC's future.

I. A Question of Momentum

Twenty years ago, a Midwestern high-research university hired me to coordinate writing across the curriculum (WAC). The College of Liberal Arts and Sciences (CLAS) and the English department contracted my position as a joint hire. I had a small but adequate start-up budget. English sent me up for tenure as associate professor during my second year, based on my experience and publications. According to Thaiss and Porter's (2010) national survey of WAC programs, these conditions augured well for the security I needed to recover and develop a program that two predecessors had attempted to establish (pp. 540–542).

However, my campus's state of writing support, my college's changing priorities, and my department's programmatic needs impinged on the leadership role I envisioned. I sometimes chose and other times got drafted into contiguous roles—a writing-center director, a participant in a partnership with a local school district, an assessment consultant, an acting director of first-year composition, an undergraduate studies director, a general-education taskforce consultant, and most recently, acting chair of English. This mélange of roles still provided many opportunities to take on substantial WAC projects, such as building a viable university writing center (UWC); bringing WAC to low-income schools; creating departmental cultures of writing and evidence; collaborating on programmatic portfolio assessments; and establishing an upper-division writing requirement in the undergraduate curriculum.

Cox, Galin and Melzer (2018) observe that leaders in such circumstances may tend to mimic "elements of other programs and use a trial-and-error approach to program development" (p. 65). What kind of WAC program does this approach produce? Is it sustainable? And if so, *how* might a university—and a WAC coordinator—sustain it? WAC's accomplishments and struggles at my university speak to these questions.

I will look at these questions through the lens of Cox et al.'s whole-systems theory. Cox et al. intend their theory to provide a structured approach toward developing new WAC programs. However, I propose an adaptive use of their theory that can also enable long-term WAC coordinators to describe a program's history, placing it in a coherent and information-rich institutional context that foregrounds ongoing formative assessment, tracks programmatic improvements, and clarifies a program's earlier trajectory. I therefore suggest that this theory is flexible enough to make a WAC program's history more readily available at critical moments when a program has veered too closely to the boundaries of what Cox et al. call a "band of equilibrium" (pp. 134-135) so that WAC coordinators, program stakeholders, and upper-level administrators can review what kinds of action have served a program well in the past and what kinds of problems they should avoid repeating.[1] I believe this case study will prove instructive for other WAC programs. But first I'll review the scholarship that informed program development at my university, previous to the advent of whole-systems theory.

According to a taxonomy that Condon and Rutz construct from "actual characteristics of existing programs," WAC at my university reflects elements that stretch sporadically across three of four program types they identify (p. 361). Even after twenty years, for example, the program might only be categorized as *foundational* because it depends mostly upon my energy as a leader and focuses largely on the schedule of workshops I conduct. It draws a loyal though slow-growing range of practitioners who apply writing to learn and learning to write (pp. 362–363).

Yet I could argue that the program is *established* because the university has expanded WAC to upper-division courses that come from the whole curriculum.

---

1. A "band of equilibrium" reveals when a WAC program possesses or lacks the sufficient resources, support, or capacity to remain stable, as measured by indicators that can demonstrate that program's sustainability.

Our offices of Faculty Development and Assessment Services as well as many department chairs, deans, and other program directors recognize WAC's campus presence. WAC has participated in influential committees and has helped shape the university's student-learning outcomes (pp. 362–363).

Yet again, the program might claim to be *integrated* within the university's various systems because it has joined three externally funded, multi-million-dollar research projects. At critical points, it has attained substantial budget growth to train faculty and expand writing-center staff. WAC has contributed to our institution's accreditation and participated in our upper-level administration's quality-enhancement projects. It has designed large-scale assessment projects with multiple benchmarks. Participants publish on WAC in their own disciplines (pp. 362–363).

But Condon and Rutz stipulate that WAC adds up to much more than this checklist of elements (p. 360). WAC must demonstrate "a complex partnership among faculty, administrators, writing centers, faculty development programs—an infrastructure that may well support general education or first-year seminar goals" (pp. 357–358). Thus, a bona fide program "can describe where it is headed" and "make decisions about the future of that program" based on how its *momentum* aligns with the institution's trajectory (pp. 360–361, my emphasis). *Momentum* so-described leads toward the fourth program-type in their taxonomy: *change agent*.

WAC as a change-agent philosophically and culturally transforms curriculum, faculty, and a university's matrix of social, economic, and institutional systems. It yields an identity for WAC that reflects the institution's other curricular supports and initiatives. It aligns with and influences the institution's multiple efforts to improve the quality of teaching and learning, and—as in *some* academic units at my university—it fully theorizes its strategic plans through scholarly research, publication, and actual practice (pp. 362–363).

While this taxonomy provides a fine-grained description of WAC-program development, Cox et al. point out that we have lacked a theoretical framework to explain and strategize WAC's momentum from foundational to change agent (p. 1). The most well-articulated theory for decades came from Walvoord's (1996) adaptation of social movement theory to WAC. She critiqued WAC's vague goals and outcomes, urging proponents to confront challenges at the micro-level (in foundational programs) and the macro-level (in established or integrated programs). At the micro-level, she urged WAC leadership to re-examine WAC-faculty membership, workshops, and follow-up to support faculty's ongoing growth, to direct them toward "a network, a culture" for spreading WAC's influence (p. 72). At the macro-level, she said WAC leaders should work with other institutional initiatives, relate to administration, understand the impact of technology, and above all, "deal with assessment" (pp. 67–74). Although this critique has helped many institutions develop

WAC—including mine—Walvoord (2018) concedes that it remained "limited as a framework for building transformative and sustainable WAC programs" (p. ix).

As a result, Cox et al. observe that "WAC programs fail to survive at an alarming rate of more than 50%" (p. 1). To grapple with this failure rate, Cox et al. propose that whole-systems theory provides a framework for "creating and assessing change" in the dynamic complexities that affect a university's approaches to teaching and learning (p. 25). Whole-systems theory advocates studying an institution's *social networks, systems,* and *capacity for resilience* to guide WAC leadership, gain insights about WAC's development, and gauge WAC's sustainability (p. 25). Studying *social networks* of students, faculty, administrators, and board members helps WAC administrators understand "the network of communications" among these institutional stakeholders so they can identify people who may "serve as conduits and/or bottlenecks" in program development (p. 25). Studying the institution's *systems* shows where in its organizational structures WAC leaders can find "leverage points . . . to make small changes that lead to significant impacts" (p. 25). Studying the institution's *capacity for resilience* can help administrators see how it handles stresses that change brings to its networks and structures, "yet maintain a relatively stable state"—while avoiding points where WAC could cross "a critical threshold" that may result in undesirable competition with other programs for resources and status (p. 25).

Accordingly, whole-systems theory can explain WAC's momentum in individual universities such as mine by analyzing its principles of

- Wholeness "as a significant intervention in a complex system"
- Broad participation, "engaging stakeholders from all levels"
- Transformational change "at multiple levels" in the system
- Resilience "to program challenges"
- Equity, minimizing disparities among "WAC faculty and student writers"
- Leadership, with the authority to plan, develop, and assess WAC
- Systematic development, with "a clear mission and prioritized goals"
- Integration "into existing structures and practices"
- Visibility "through multiple means of reporting"
- Feedback, to inform decision-making, program balance, and WAC-project sustainability (pp. 46–47)

Keeping these principles in mind, WAC leadership can deploy a methodology for initiating and sustaining project-based momentum that begins with *understanding* (which maps the campus mood and its ideological constructs toward writing), proceeds to *planning* (which involves identifying stakeholders, gathering their support, and setting WAC's mission), and moves on to *developing* (which identifies sustainability indicators for WAC projects and uses them to measure successful implementation

(p. 55). Within this methodology, *leading* entails management of program growth and change through assessment, improvement, and communication (p. 55).

Equipped with a theory and method that encompass such a scope, WAC leadership can "look at data collected across time" and ask, "What do these data tell you about the ways the program has changed and grown? Has the program turned any indicators of distress into indicators of success? What could be adjusted to keep the program resilient"? (p. 198). Just so, whole-systems theory offers a systemic approach not only to program-building and sustainment but to evaluating WAC's *institutional history* as well. Evaluating WAC's history helps its leadership look back so it can think ahead.

In the following case study, I shape what Cox et al. call "sustainability indicators" into a sample rubric that can help WAC leadership read its institutional history. I then use this rubric to assess WAC's momentum during three periods at my university: program-building, decline, and recovery. I conclude with a reflection on what such a historical reading of a program might tell its institution, its stakeholders, and its leadership about WAC's sustainability.

II. A Tool to Gauge WAC's Momentum

Cox et al. say that a whole-systems approach grounds program development in "discrete projects that work through cycles of planning, doing, checking, and improving using *sustainability indicators* (SIs) to monitor progress" (pp. 25–26, my emphasis). They assert that this approach emphasizes formative, not summative assessment—as well as programmatic improvements, not quantified proofs of programmatic efficacy. But years of submitting reports on UWC and WAC data have taught me that faculty, committees, and administrators who agree to implement WAC also want quantifiable information about *every* project a WAC program conducts so as to establish a tenable number of writing-intensive (WI) courses throughout the curriculum. The information they seek breaks into data points that look a lot like SIs:

- Departments and programs with potential or existing WI courses
- Capacity of student support to grow WI courses
- Amount of faculty support needed to grow WI courses
- Equitable numbers of faculty willing to teach WI courses
- Budget capacity to support WI courses
- Capacity to assess and improve WI courses
- Control of class size for WI courses
- Capacity of a university committee to oversee WI courses
- Capacity of a WAC coordinator to manage WI courses
- Communications to promote WAC-program visibility

Cox et al. also identify many of these data points as potential SIs (pp. 152–153). Extrapolating SIs in such a manner does not meet Cox et al.'s ideal of collaborating directly with WAC stakeholders to determine what SIs to use. But extrapolating what faculty, committees, and administrators repeatedly request goes far in "establishing baseline SIs" that determine "which actions will be sustainable" when assessing the momentum and vulnerabilities of WI courses (p. 56). Concurrently, I suggest a six-point scale for each SI as: minimal, fair, moderate, sufficient, good, and substantial. Within this scale, I adopt what Cox et al. call "a range within which actions will be sustainable"—or a "band of equilibrium" of 1–5 (p. 56).

Although no specific collaboration occurred at my university with the SIs identified above, a committee of cross-curricular faculty and I indeed collaborated on what defines WI courses. Before we proposed to establish a two-course upper-division baccalaureate writing requirement at our university, we agreed that such courses should cap enrollment at 35 and require final approval from the university's General Education Committee. Writing should count for at least 25% of the grade. Each student should meet a minimum of 3,000 words. Faculty must conduct class discussions about their writing assignments and provide substantive, on-going feedback (perhaps in concert with the UWC). Faculty teaching WI courses must also obtain prior approval from department chairs so if others teach the same course, they must satisfy the requirements too.

The above SIs and definition of WI have enabled me to design the rubric in Table 1.

Table 1.

Sustainability Scales for WAC

Degree Programs*	Student Support*
Minimum (10-15% w/ 1-2 WI courses) **Fair** (15-25% w/ 1-2 courses) **Moderate** (25-50% w/ 1-3 courses) **Sufficient** (50-65% w/ 3 or more courses) **Good** (65-80% w/ 5 or more courses) **Substantial** (above 80% w/ 5 or more courses) *~140 combined undergraduate and graduate programs	**Minimum** (UWC or equivalent capacity for 1–2% of undergraduate enrollment) **Fair** (as above for 2-5% of undergraduate and graduate enrollment + adequate tutor-training) **Moderate** (as above for 5-10% of enrollment + well-focused, credit-bearing tutor training that includes work with English-as second-language students) **Sufficient** (as above for 10-15% of enrollment) **Good** (as above for 15-25% of enrollment) **Substantial** (as above for 25-33% of enrollment) *Assume < 5% annual users turned away

Faculty Support	Equitable Number of Faculty to Teach WI*
Minimum (UWC or other supplemental writing instruction) **Fair** (as above + 1–2 major workshops) **Moderate** (as above + workshop series + in-class support + assessment projects + faculty incentives) **Sufficient** (as above + faculty department and program leaders + administrative commitment of resources) **Good** (as above + university-wide assessment) **Substantial** (as above + support for WAC research)	**Minimum** (8-10% of instructional faculty; over half in FYC and general education in English) **Fair** (10-20% of instructional faculty, at least 1/3 professorial) **Moderate** (20–35% of all instructional faculty) **Sufficient** (35–60% of all instructional faculty) **Good** (60–75% of all instructional faculty) **Substantial** (75% or more of all instructional faculty) *Includes TAs and instructors in FYC
Budget Capacity	**Capacity to Assess**
Minimum (paid/reassigned staff that meets student demand for UWC services) **Fair** (as above + dedicated position for UWC director + funds for tutoring supplies and UWC publicity/outreach) **Moderate** (as above + tenurable/continuous position for UWC/WAC director(s) + discretionary funds for faculty workshops) **Sufficient** (as above + access to grants/ resources + assessment funds + research support) **Good** (as above + scheduled institutional replacement cycle for technology and equipment) **Substantial** (as above + in-built support for UWC/WAC staff expansion and pay upgrades)	**Minimum** (UWC feedback to students and faculty on tutorial help with writing skills relevant to FYC outcomes) **Fair** (as above + UWC assessment projects/ reports on student skills) **Moderate** (as above + documented WAC influence on assessing disciplinary writing skills in academic departments' learning outcomes) **Sufficient** (as above + documented WAC influence on assessment projects measuring writing skills embedded in institution's baccalaureate learning outcomes) **Good** (as above + WAC leadership in continuous assessment projects that assess individual degree-program writing outcomes) **Substantial** (as above + participation in assessment projects through coalitions, disciplinary organizations and publications)

Control of Class Size	**Committee Oversight**
Minimum (faculty decide which classes are WI-appropriate) **Fair** (departments and program directors set caps for writing courses, per college's' approval) **Moderate** (as above, but using class-size limits comparable to caps that other institutions set) **Sufficient** (limits recommended in agreement with National Council of Teachers of English) **Good** (as above, with limits established for all WI courses by a standing university committee) **Substantial** (as above, with resources to protect and sustain class-size limits)	**Minimum** (small faculty group that collaborates occasionally with supplemental-writing staff) **Fair** (ad hoc committee formed as a task force to address WAC issues) **Moderate** (standing college/university committee that receives UWC/WAC reports on a regular basis) **Sufficient** (standing university committee that evaluates WAC courses and WAC/UWC reports) **Good** (as above + capacity to reward progress or respond to WAC/UWC issues + supervision of relevant projects) **Substantial** (as above + ability to negotiate curricular policies in colleges, departments and programs + recommend resource allocations for WAC/UWC)
Coordinator's Course-Management	**Program Visibility**
Minimum (6-8 weekly hours for micro-level WAC duties—e.g., designing and conducting workshops and follow-up activities) **Fair** (as above + opportunity to develop/teach for-credit undergraduate/graduate courses in WAC pedagogy) **Moderate** (as above + recognized role as WAC consultant in assessment and curricular decision-making at departmental and programmatic levels) **Sufficient** (as above + recognized as participant in curricular decision-making at institutional level) **Good** (as above + defined role in standing committee or office that assesses curriculum at institutional level) **Substantial** (as above + role in deciding assessment-based institutional actions/policies)	**Minimum** (website/materials to promote services) **Fair** (as above + online resources for faculty and students) **Moderate** (as above + alliances with other student services and professional development projects) **Sufficient** (as above + campus-wide recognition as an institutional teaching and learning asset + scholarly publications) **Good** (as above + strong reporting lines to multiple institutional systems) **Substantial** (as above + recognition of WAC as a source of institutional data that contributes to decision-making)

To illustrate how this rubric can help assess WAC's history, I begin with my first year of hire. Table 2's overview shows where WAC had succeeded, where it failed, and what remained.

Table 2.

Baseline Indicators for Development (Year 1)

INDICATORS	SPECIFIC DETAILS
Degree programs with existing/potential WI courses	39 degree programs (per writing-center documentation)
Capacity of student support to grow WI courses	8 writing fellows assigned to 6 departments in 3 colleges (350-400 total sessions annually) Writing center (~1,200 sessions annually) Total WF/WC visitors > 1% undergraduate enrollment
Amount of faculty support needed to grow WI courses	Previous workshops/faculty retreats discontinued Consultations sporadic
Equitable number of faculty willing to teach WI courses	~50 faculty across 6 colleges, ~39 departments and programs Instructors and TAs primarily in First-Year Composition
Capacity to assess and improve WI Courses	No formal UWC documentation of tutorial feedback No clear WAC connection to assessing WI courses One TA consistently reported back to English
Budget capacity to support WI courses (training, assessment, resources)	Funding for 8 writing fellows (1-2 course assignments each) 2.5 FTE FYC instructors/TAs reassigned to writing center (10 course assignments); funding for 6 to 8 peer tutors
Control of class size for WI courses	Faculty decision
Capacity of a university committee to oversee WI courses	No committee; small faculty core who support WAC
Capacity of WAC coordinator to manage WI courses	2 course releases for a non-tenured instructor to oversee a small writing center 1 course release for another instructor to supervise writing fellows
Communications to promote WAC program visibility	Newsletter for 5 departments (WAC TA, editor) WAC website (maintained by WAC TAs) 1 TA's annual report on WAC in five departments, sent to CLAS dean and English Chair

Table 2 consolidates writing-center data to suggest how previous workshops and consultations had raised faculty awareness in approximately 39 (or 27%) of the university's ~140 degree programs—implying that the campus was receptive to WAC. Even so, only about 50 professors, non-tenured instructors, and TAs currently assigned writing that motivated ~1,200 annual student visits to the writing center. First-year composition accounted for most. Neither students nor faculty received documentation of tutors' feedback. A "culture of writing" had yet to take hold where: 1) a faculty majority valued writing and practiced effective assignment design; 2) departments included writing to assess degree-program outcomes; and 3) the university expected degree-programs to report such outcomes in review cycles.

The concept of WAC as a program had become nebulous. A non-tenured FYC instructor received a two-course reassignment from his four-course load to oversee a writing-center staff of instructors, TAs, and undergraduate students. But he felt unprepared to train them. Another non-tenured FYC instructor received one course release to supervise six English TAs and two psychology TAs who served as writing fellows in various departments. But her efforts to engage more professorial faculty met with scant response. Individual writing-fellows "guesstimated" that they handled 40 to 50 undergraduate sessions per year. One writing fellow issued a WAC newsletter regularly to the departments of economics, history, political science, psychology, and sociology. Other English writing fellows helped maintain a WAC website with tips for assigning and responding to student writing. These communicative structures made WAC visible, but programmatic interconnectivity had nearly withered.

Table 2 captures this situation, but as Cox et al. suggest, radar charts such as Figure 1 provide administrators and stakeholders with a more easily grasped measure of "how all SIs for . . . a WI program can be mapped together" (p. 151). Figure 1 identifies a minimal number of faculty and students accounted for this situation. The chart reveals minimum budgeting capacity to expand WAC and a somewhat fair communication effort to raise WAC's visibility. But with no committee to review syllabi or advocate for enrollment limits, WAC-influenced courses ranged as high as 500 or as low as 10. Taken together, Figure 1's map of WAC's sustainability yields a calculation of .75—a program clinging to the inner boundary of the band of equilibrium, very near to its demise.

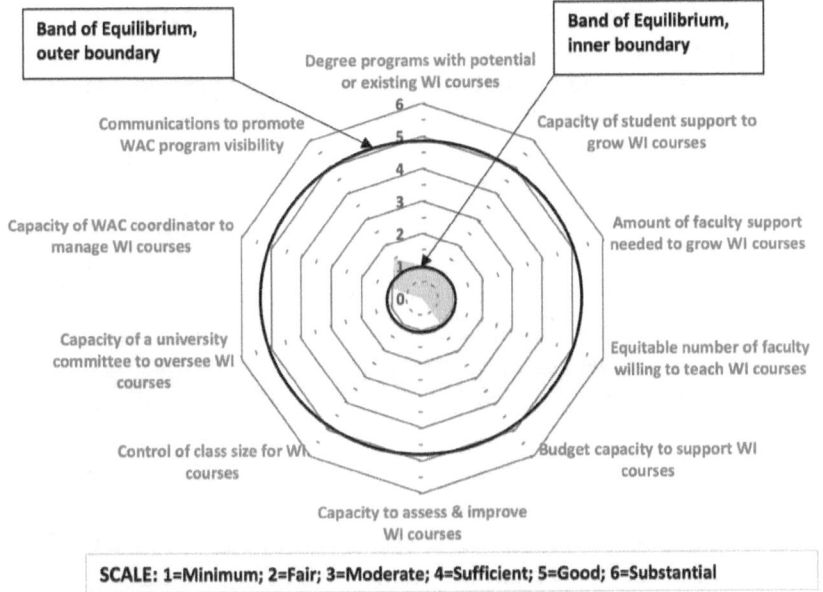

Figure 1. Baseline chart of WAC program sustainability.

Cox et al. recommend that such charts offer "a negative feedback loop mechanism" which points to "interventions when conditions warrant change" (p. 151). Although I had no such chart to illustrate it, in year one I told supporters in CLAS and English that WAC must first set up a viable writing center. Without it, WAC would have no future.

III. Measuring History: Five Years of Momentum

Cox et al. aver that WAC programs which "take a deliberate project approach are predictably more viable over time" (154). Everything depends, however, on *which* projects should take precedence. Our initial project to build up a viable UWC would provide maximum leverage for WAC because the existing cubby-hole in the English department would never serve the university—even at its lowest point of enrollment.[2] Furthermore, transforming a sleepy little writing center into the mainstay for

---

2. The campus *Data Book* (2018) shows at that point, we had 60 undergraduate and 80 graduate degree programs, 12,788 undergraduates, 4,121 graduates, 654 tenured or tenure-track faculty, 523 instructional faculty, and 1,319 graduate assistants (p. 82).

WI courses would help us grasp "the complexity of the [university's] system[s] and its curricular ecology" (see Cox et al., p. 154).

When English colleagues and an associate dean agreed to get behind the UWC project, I assumed its directorship. A small staff of instructors, graduate assistants, undergraduate tutors, and I ventured into classrooms campus-wide. Many faculty expressed surprise that a place existed where their students could get extra writing instruction. So we got the message out. In addition, an increased schedule of WAC workshops helped draw together a "grassroots network of faculty" who discussed and implemented WAC pedagogy and lent support to "WAC policies and initiatives" (Cox et al., p. 156). The trickle of students coming to the writing center became an overflow. However, we did not yet understand the campus culture of writing well enough to formulate what Cox and Galin (2020) call "'baseline SIs,' which could be used for planning interventions and assessing their impact" (p. 43).

A group of invested professors who represented each of the university's colleges agreed to convene as a WAC advisory committee to help turn the writing center's overflow problem into an opportunity. With the committee's input, I wrote a WAC self-study to request an external consultant-evaluators' visit from the Council of Writing Program Administrators (see McLeod 1991, pp. 73-75; Brady 2004, pp. 85-86). The self-study helped us better understand aspects of the campus writing culture, including where hubs of faculty concern about writing were located—and how institutional power was distributed across campus (see Cox & Galin, p. 43). A rudimentary WAC mission and a sense of programmatic goals began to coalesce: WAC and the UWC would aim to support faculty and students in the university's efforts to improve teaching and learning, especially by promoting the growth of WAC-informed courses. Thus, the advisory committee, the associate dean, and my English-department colleagues helped me plan a UWC project that could accommodate the whole campus and pull WAC's sustainability into the band of equilibrium that Figure 1 illustrates. The CLAS dean approved. He especially appreciated that the external CWPA team would help us form productive connections with other colleges and upper-level administrators throughout the university, while also performing functions similar to those of an accreditation agency (see "Consultant-Evaluator Service," 2020).

As this "macro-level" project garnered interest that reached "the higher scales of departments, colleges, academic senate, [and] institutional assessment," WAC became a university-wide concern, making "strategic interventions" into its complex social, economic, and institutional systems (see Cox et al., pp. 58, 157-158). Following the CWPA visit, the provost helped us shape the UWC project into a plan that we submitted to the state's Board of Higher Education. In a year, we received $190,000 annual funding to initiate the UWC's construction. These advances poised

WAC to make a substantive curricular footprint. From UWC records of student sessions and faculty assignments, we saw that workshop participants, newsletters, and the redesigned WAC/UWC website were spreading WAC pedagogy even to faculty who didn't attend WAC events.

When we moved into the new UWC (complete with tutoring areas, a smart classroom, meeting space, offices, bathrooms, and a kitchenette), construction funds converted into a budget for expanding staff and faculty outreach. The university's Assessment Office helped us initiate a University Writing Project to evaluate "WAC faculty's" student learning outcomes (SLOs), and I held workshops at other campus initiatives such as our Multicultural Institute. The School of Nursing asked me to help with their portfolio effort, which became a long-lived campus model for authentic assessment of WAC. The College of Business requested a year-long series of workshops to revise their departmental writing outcomes. A WAC-Advisory Committee member convinced me to join her National Science Foundation project in an urban school district, where I introduced WAC to high-school teachers. Research and publications emerged.

Table 3 provides more details of WAC's momentum during this period.

Table 3.

WAC Sustainability During the UWC Project (Years 1-5)

INDICATORS	SPECIFIC DETAILS
Degree programs with existing/potential WI courses	Increase from 39 to 51 degree programs annually
Capacity of student support to grow WI courses	New UWC established Class visits and in-class assignment workshops begun UWC's smart classroom constructed for FYC courses 2.5 FTE English instructors/TAs reassigned to UWC; writing fellows converted to UWC tutors Increase from ~1,700 to 7,714 sessions (12% of university enrollment) Credit-bearing undergraduate/graduate courses developed to train peer tutors/TAs in WAC/UWC pedagogy
Amount of faculty support needed to grow WI courses	10-15 faculty workshops offered annually Annual day-long faculty workshop initiated in May 25-40 faculty consultations annually Discipline-specific workshops for Nursing and College of Business
Equitable number of faculty willing to teach WI courses	Increase from ~50 to 645 professors, instructors and TAs across 7 colleges (including Law) Increase in UWC staff's ethnic diversity and majors WAC's participation in university's Multicultural Institute

INDICATORS	SPECIFIC DETAILS
Capacity to assess and improve WI Courses	WAC self-study for CWPA consultant-evaluator visit Portfolio assessment developed in baccalaureate Nursing degree University Writing Project (UWP) assessment of WI-course outcomes initiated 2-year UWC assessment of ~800 multiple-draft writers conducted
Budget capacity to support WI courses (training, assessment, resources)	Funding for writing fellows converted to UWC staffing funds New funding stream to add UWC staff positions (associate director, 1 FTE instructor and ~25 peer tutors) 2-3 annual WAC grants for department and faculty projects WAC stipends established for May workshop participants WAC grant to develop Nursing portfolio Assessment Office funds for UWP Funds set aside to assess UWC outcomes NSF-grant funds to develop workshops and teach graduate-level WAC courses for high/middle-school teachers
Control of class size for WI courses	Faculty decision—but WI-course caps discussed in WAC Advisory Committee
Capacity of a university committee to oversee WI	WAC Advisory Committee established to support WAC and advocate for construction of new UWC Increased WAC-Advisory influence on departments and colleges NSF-grant committee to plan high/middle-school outreach
Capacity of WAC coordinator to manage WI courses	Per-semester course release to coordinate WAC and direct UWC (~15 hrs./week) Bi-weekly meetings with Nursing Portfolio Committee Bi-weekly involvement with NSF high/middle-school project Credit-bearing undergrad/grad courses and independent studies developed for UWC tutoring and WAC pedagogy
Communications to promote WAC program visibility	70-100 annual "brochure talks" in cross-disciplinary classes Newsletter for all departments, 6 colleges (WAC coordinator, editor) UWC website updated (WAC coordinator, webmaster) Annual reports to CLAS and English Chair (WAC coordinator, compiler) Scholarship on UWC methods and WAC outcomes

Moving from Table 3 to Figure 2, WAC/UWC data show a moderate growth in departments and degree programs with potential or existing WAC-informed courses. The moderate increase in WAC workshops parallels the increase among faculty who encouraged students to use the UWC. WAC's participation in the university's annual Multicultural Institute brought a fair rise in diversity among professorial faculty, instructors, and cross-disciplinary TAs willing to teach WI courses. A sufficient budget allowed us to develop a two-year assessment project to measure UWC SLOs in 802 student folders containing multiple drafts of writing assignments. We estimated that our capacity to help students improve their performance in WI courses was approaching a moderate level. Our budget also exerted a moderate impact on increased campus outreach and communications. More staff also yielded more class visits and in-class workshops, moderately increasing WAC's capacity to manage WI courses. I initiated WAC/UWC-training courses and did independent studies for peer tutors and graduate students. Figure 2 thus maps how WAC's engagement on the macro-level affects program development.

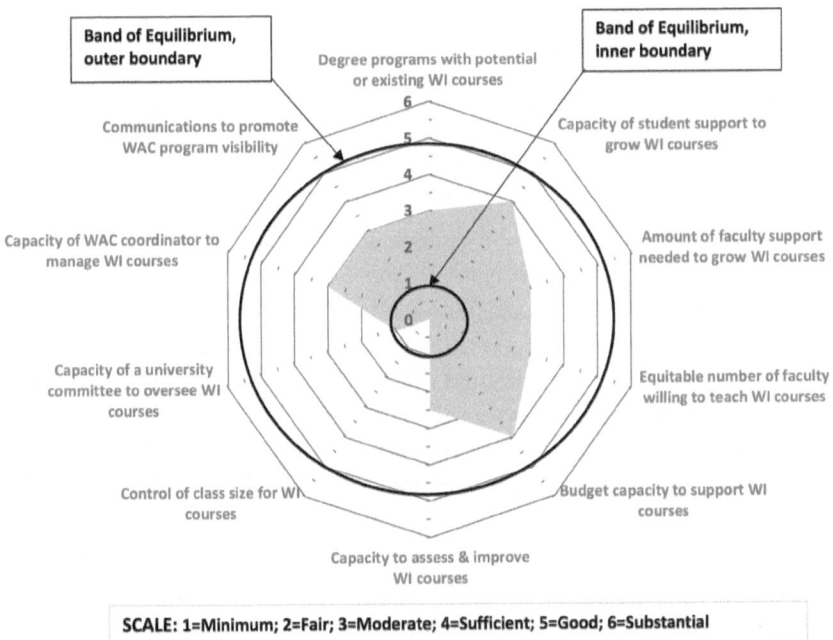

Figure 2. Impact of a well-funded UWC on WAC program sustainability

But assessing the improvements that our UWC project exerted upon WAC also shows where momentum lagged. The advisory committee served WAC well in helping us establish the UWC, but still the university regarded it as an ad hoc entity.

The committee did not have the institutional clout to propose baccalaureate writing requirements in upper-division courses in the major or exert controls on enrollments in WAC-informed courses. These factors had a negative impact on faculty willing to implement WAC pedagogy more fully. Nor had we formulated what Cox and Galin identify as "proto SIs" to gauge internally how we could more closely align our rudimentary program mission and goals with what the upper-level administration expected from us externally (p. 43). The administration had set benchmarks that would satisfy protocols for annual and eight-year review cycles (e.g., appropriate increase in number of students served, clear documentation of contact hours, cost-effective use of resources for staffing, adequate outreach to academic units, substantial signs of faculty satisfaction, and ideally, measurable impact upon SLOs). Accordingly, Figure 2 suggests that the WAC program's sustainability score had nearly risen to moderate (2.65)—a promising trend, yet one that encountered barriers and implied that we had yet to establish a stable means to strategize and safeguard that sustainability within the band of equilibrium that the rubric gauges.

IV. Assessing Decline: The Next Six Years

Universities undergo constant change. WAC stakeholders come and go as priorities shift. Institutional memory falls prey to amnesia if WAC leadership does not keep its projects in sight of faculty and administrators, working "at both the micro and macro levels" (Cox et al., p. 156).

Ironically, WAC's decline came about because of its expansion. An undergraduate English course on WAC drew increasingly more students from different bachelors-degree programs. I developed a graduate seminar to train advanced English TAs to teach multiple sections of the course and assess the course portfolios with a rubric I'd refined from a university workshop on the national VALUE Rubric Development Project (see Association of American Colleges and Universities 2010). I took on more independent studies, theses, and dissertations focused on WAC. The portfolio-assessment project in the School of Nursing thrived, and its faculty requested frequent workshops. When the NSA grant ended, CLAS and the College of Education obtained federal and state grants to continue the school-district partnership. The CLAS dean assigned me to set up WAC resources in partner schools. I developed a graduate-level course for high-school teachers that I taught onsite for several semesters. As my department chair urged me to publish more so I could be promoted to full professor, the onsite school-district courses led me into research projects—including one with a high-school science department. The first-year composition director and I co-wrote a successful application to join the Inter/National Coalition for Electronic Portfolio Research (I/NCEPR, 2017) for three years. But these over-commitments cannibalized my release-time for WAC.

As Cox et al. would put it, I joined other WAC leaders who get "overwhelmed by ever-expanding micro-level demands" (p. 156).

Trusting that the UWC would provide ample support for WAC-informed courses, I gave up its directorship to pursue multiplying WAC projects. The associate director—an English MA—replaced me. This change weakened the connections WAC had made at the macro level. The WAC Advisory Committee disbanded. The University Writing Project continued, but with fewer faculty contributors from WAC workshops. More problematic, a hostile dean replaced our friendly one. He viewed WAC and writing centers as a misdirected use of resources. With my energies focused elsewhere, the UWC became the target of budget cuts and staff reductions, increasing the UWC director's workload. A replacement cycle for the UWC's smart-classroom technology fell by the wayside.

Cox et al. warn that if a program never moves on from—or retreats to—an overconcern with micro-level work, WAC becomes "difficult to sustain, and may never get to the tipping point where it has a transformative effect on the campus culture of writing (p. 156). Table 4 details six years, during which WAC tipped far away from campus transformation.

Table 4.

WAC Sustainability During School-District Partnership and Budget Cuts (Years 6-11)

INDICATORS	SPECIFIC DETAILS
Degree programs with existing/ potential WI courses	Decrease from 72 to 41 degree programs across 6 colleges annually
Capacity of student support to grow WI courses	UWC services strained Continued in-class visits and assignment workshops (70-100 annually) UWC smart-classroom accommodation for FYC courses hampered by outdated technology Continued 2.5 FTE reassignment of English TAs in UWC Decreased UWC visitors (12%→9% of university enrollment) and increased number of sessions (7,714→9,390); 749→1,683 students turned away annually Continued credit-bearing courses to prepare TAs as UWC tutors and instructors in English WAC course

INDICATORS	SPECIFIC DETAILS
Amount of faculty support needed to grow WI courses	2 FTE instructors in UWC eliminated and peer tutors reduced 50% 2 continued day-long faculty workshops in May (one on academic publishing) Continued workshops for Nursing 8-10 WAC consultations with university faculty annually
Equitable number of faculty willing to teach WI courses	Decrease, 645→464 professors, instructors and TAs Discontinued WAC participation in Multicultural Institute
Capacity to assess and improve WI Courses	Continued WI course assessment by University Writing Project Continued Nursing baccalaureate-degree portfolio assessment Continued portfolio assessment of English WAC course WAC-assessment research in high-school partnership
Budget capacity to support WI courses (training, assessment, resources)	Decrease in college budget for UWC staff Reduced WAC stipends for faculty in May workshop WI course assessment funded by University Assessment Office—team of English instructors paid Continued grant funds for courses in WAC instruction and research for high-school partnership
Control of class size for WI courses	Faculty decision
Capacity of a university committee to oversee WAC	WAC Advisory Committee disbanded
Capacity of WAC coordinator to manage WI courses	Course releases replaced by onsite courses in high-school partnership Management time redirected to WI courses and research in high schools Oversight of credit-bearing English course on WAC—4 sections annually
Communications to promote WAC program visibility	Separate UWC and WAC websites (maintained by UWC director and WAC coordinator) Continued annual WAC and UWC reports to dean, English chair Continued scholarship on WAC in secondary schools and Nursing portfolio-assessment

With a shrinking staff, the UWC director limited student sessions to 30 minutes to meet a fair level of undergraduate and graduate student need. She visited an average of 70 to 100 classrooms per year to do UWC "brochure talks" and assignment workshops. Thus, a fair number of departments and programs kept sending students, despite alarming percentages of turn-aways at busy times such as midterm and the semester's end. Turn-aways caused the number of faculty and degree programs offering WAC-informed courses to creep downward toward fair. My work with the university's school-district partnership meant minimal oversight of WAC-informed courses on campus. Faculty support in WAC dwindled to two day-long May workshops and discipline-specific workshops for Nursing. Figure 3 reflects as much.

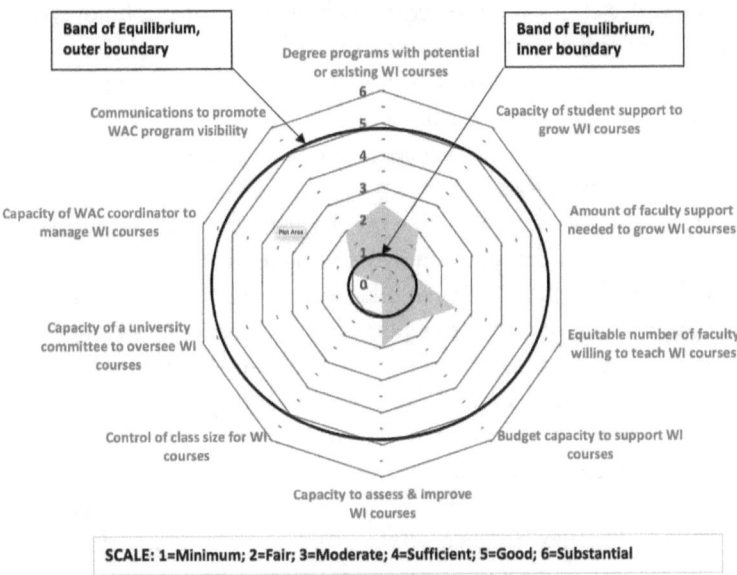

Figure 3. WAC decline during school-district partnership and CLAS budget cuts

As budget cuts continued, UWC staffing lost two fulltime instructors. The dean allowed the UWC director to convert one instructor's salary into peer-tutoring funds, but the other's salary disappeared along with half of the UWC's budget. The absence of a WAC advisory committee didn't help. Professorial faculty no longer had a representative body to contact when the UWC was forced to turn their students away. And although the UWC and WAC continued to submit annual reports, the hostile dean disregarded them either as requests for support that he did not want to give or activities that focused more on high-school teachers than university faculty. As the UWC and WAC websites grew outdated, communication lines grew quieter.

As such, Figure 3 reveals a WAC program whose six-year contraction rendered sustainability lower than "fair" (1.45). SIs crept down toward the inner boundary of the band of equilibrium. The program had destabilized.

V. Project-Based Interventions: A Nine-Year Turn-Around

Cox et al. observe cases where faculty demand for WAC support remains high but is met only by a writing center. They say such support, crucial as it is, does not result "in a robust culture of writing" or give faculty the incentive to sustain—let alone develop—WI courses (p. 150). WAC's six-year decline at my university tends to confirm, but what could be done? Cox et al. argue that recovery requires "project-based intervention, with a clear set of problems, a clear set of targeted solutions, transparent lines of WAC leadership, and a grassroots approach to change" (150).

The next nine-year period substantiates Cox et al.'s argument. Our university orchestrated a concatenation of quality-enhancement projects. WAC's shift back to a macro-level focus occurred as it participated. This participation added up to a series of project-based interventions.

Recovery began unexpectedly when my department asked me to assume acting directorship of first-year composition. My colleague needed a break to work on his promotion. Thereafter, the assessment office contacted me for a report on the FYC SLOs that our research project with e-portfolios had produced. I requested a year to collect data that could tie together FYC SLOs and upper-division WAC outcomes from the University Writing Project. The assessment office asked me to prepare a presentation for the board of trustees. I did so. At the end of that presentation, the provost proclaimed that the continuum of FYC to WAC, with the UWC assisting, was "really a prototype for things as we develop baccalaureate goals and look at revising general education" (Banks-Wilkins, 2009, p. 9). Ears pricked up. Change was afoot.

Later, the provost issued a university-wide call to submit proposals for Strategic Initiative Projects to support curricular quality-enhancement. When I contacted the UWC director and learned the full extent of damage that budget cuts had wreaked, we teamed up to write a proposal. The hostile dean saw an opportunity to shift CLAS's funding burden for the UWC to the provost's office. He supported our proposal, and it got accepted.

Our Strategic Initiatives proposal morphed into a five-year "Vision Project." We received a combined $82,500 annual funding for UWC and WAC. If our annual reports to the Vision Committee and the dean proved convincing, we could receive a permanent addition to our budgets—nearly replacing the cuts the dean had made. UWC numbers and services gradually improved. Turn-aways dropped. Run-down technology in the UWC smart classroom got replaced. WAC workshops increased again, attracting new faculty.

Nevertheless, when funds for our Vision Project ended, the hostile dean did not recommend continued UWC/WAC support. His rationale: little curricular change, no evidence of improved learning, and too much drain on more worthwhile projects. He cut the UWC budget even further and eliminated WAC's budget altogether.

Cox et al. advise WAC administrators "to take a systems approach to [such] challenges, which includes not taking things personally, exercising patience, listening carefully, thinking logically, and using common sense when dealing with conflicts" (p. 164). This approach includes "collection of any necessary data, consideration of the scope of its reach, attention to primary stakeholders, a desire to balance the concerns that need to be considered, and a willingness to be flexible" (p. 164). At this time, my stint in FYC ended. My department asked me to direct its undergraduate studies program. The FYC directorship had taught me that such a position would enable me to maintain upper-level contacts I'd made and help form new ones.

Opportunities appeared. The provost appointed a Baccalaureate Review Task Force charged with researching what students, parents, alumni, employers, and other stakeholders had to say about graduating seniors' skills. Underdeveloped writing skills rose to the top of the list ("Baccalaureate Review," 2009, pp. 16-17). The provost consequently appointed another task force—including WAC-friendly members from the Vision Project and Baccalaureate Review—to revise the university's general-education program. I contacted this Task Force on Progressive Learning in Undergraduate Studies (PLUS) as well as the assessment office about WAC and the UWC. My concurrent positions in undergraduate studies and WAC elicited positive response.

We began a three-year study that funded faculty participants in WAC workshops to test and assess what they'd learned about tentative WI requirements. The assessment office gathered baseline data from FYC e-portfolio scores. Using the university's course documentation system, the assessment office identified students who took WAC-informed courses and compared them with students who did not. UWC records cross-checked data. Statistically significant gains in writing skills emerged for the undergraduates in WI courses. Sharing these results with the PLUS Task Force and the university's Academic Planning Council led to a revision of lower and upper-division general education that proposed resources to support a new university-wide definition of writing-intensive courses. The university president, in turn, agreed to move the UWC out of CLAS and put the UWC under the provost's purview so it would have adequate funding. A vice provost shopped the PLUS proposal to all the university's colleges to validate a two-course, upper-division writing requirement (PLUS Task Force, 2014, pp. 5-7). Colleges agreed, with a caveat. Faculty wanted support for developing WI courses. The Faculty Development Office (FDO) agreed to sponsor an ongoing series of faculty workshops that I would design and conduct. Upon getting the colleges' go-ahead, the university President ordered immediate implementation.

Table 5 elaborates upon these and other macro-level details of this nine-year turn-around.

Table 5.

WAC Sustainability During Vision Project, Revision of General Education and Implementation of Plus Program (Years 12–20).

INDICATORS	SPECIFIC DETAILS
Degree programs with existing/ potential WI courses	Increase, 73 degree programs across 7 colleges (including Law)
Capacity of student support to grow WI courses	Continuation of UWC services, including 70-100 in-class workshops UWC smart-classroom technology replaced Increase in UWC staff (10 TAs and 14 peer tutors) Increased UWC visitors (18% university enrollment, 12,615 sessions); turn-aways reduced to 174 Continued credit-bearing courses to prepare TAs as UWC tutors and instructors of WAC course in English (8 sections annually)
Amount of faculty support needed to grow WI courses	Increased faculty workshops annually (15-17) plus 2 daylong May workshops 20 to 35 faculty consultations annually Continued workshops for baccalaureate Nursing degree
Equitable number of faculty willing to teach WI courses	Increase, 506 professors, instructors and TAs (including Centers for Black, Latina/o, South Asian, and Women's Studies)
Capacity to assess and improve WI Courses	5-year Strategic Initiatives assessment of UWC and WAC services Continued WI-course assessment by University Writing Project Longitudinal SLO assessment of 640 WI/non-WI students Continued Nursing baccalaureate-degree portfolio assessment; portfolios initiated for RN-to-Bachelor of Nursing Continued portfolio assessment of English WAC course

INDICATORS	SPECIFIC DETAILS
Budget capacity to support WI courses (training, assessment, resources)	UWC budget shifted from CLAS to Provost and staffing resources increased FDO sponsorship of 2 daylong May workshops and new workshop series Assessment Office funds for 3-year study of SLOs in WAC classes Continued Assessment Office stipends for English instructors to score upper-division student writing
Control of class size for WI courses	Class size for WAC courses limited to 35, per upper-division baccalaureate writing requirement
Capacity of a university committee to oversee WI courses	5-year Vision Committee oversight of UWC and WAC Ad hoc committee appointed by Vice Provost to establish upper-division baccalaureate writing requirement Curriculum committees in 6 colleges to identify writing-infused courses General Education Committee to approve development of WI courses
Capacity of WAC coordinator to manage WI courses	2-year appointment as Acting First-Year Composition director, 1:1 course load 5-year appointment as director of Undergraduate Studies in English, 1:1 course load Faculty training for 3-year study of WI SLOs Collaboration with First-Year Composition and PLUS Program to incorporate WAC-specific content Collaboration with Vice Provost and cross-curricular faculty to establish upper-division baccalaureate writing requirement Collaboration with UNIV 101/201 to develop writing assignments for annual common-reading experience
Communications to promote WAC program visibility	UWC and WAC websites updated Annual WAC/UWC reports to CLAS, various task forces, Provost Presentation of FYC SLOs to Board of Trustees and Provost Presentation to University Assessment Panel, 3-year study of SLOs in WI courses Continued scholarship on WAC

During this nine-year period, the UWC recorded a moderate rise in degree programs with potential or existing WI courses. UWC budget increases allowed student support to reach a level of good. The faculty development office's sponsorship of WAC workshops helped faculty support increase to moderate. The results of the three-year project on SLOs in WI-courses sparked a moderate rise in assessment efforts, numbers of faculty willing to teach WI courses, and my capacity to manage such courses. Updates to the WAC and UWC websites, website descriptions of the PLUS Program, online catalog information about WI courses, and WAC/UWC reports submitted to various task forces and the Provost raised WAC's visibility to sufficient. Meanwhile, task forces and committees contributed to a moderate level of WI-course oversight. Moreover, the PLUS Program's revision of university baccalaureate learning outcomes led to a revision of FYC courses to include introductory WAC instruction.

As Figure 4 demonstrates, WAC reached an overall sustainability rating of 3.3—placing our program right in the middle of the band of equilibrium. Such a reading, however, can mislead. Even when a program's SIs go higher on a rubric, conditions don't necessarily get better. If more than one SI reaches "substantial," for instance, this rise may place the program in jeopardy of overcommitment and *un*sustainability. Just so, program coordinators may need to exercise caution in sharing externally all the information that internally raises hopes of ongoing equilibrium. Moreover, unanticipated changes can hit. To illustrate, a conservative governor decided to suspend the budget for our state university system for two years. The hostile dean—as well as influential and friendly supporters—left, bringing others to the fore who needed to learn about WAC. I went on sabbatical, and upon return, was asked to serve as acting department chair—adding new opportunities as well as new obligations that complicated the task of program leadership.

All of these events affect and reflect the formative nature of assessment informed by whole-systems theory. As such, our WAC program's SIs did not remain at the fortuitous levels that Figure 4 documents. But thus far, WAC's integration into the university's whole-systems structure has managed to retain moderate-to-fair programmatic stability within the band of equilibrium. Will it go on this way, despite the fluctuations? Our history warns us not to make assumptions. Hence, I suggest with caution that program coordinators elsewhere will find that whole-systems theory is invaluable to tracking their program's historical sustainability. But above all, it's important to share the data that its application can generate, to show WAC administrators and university stakeholders where to take action to protect a program's strengths and prevent its decline.

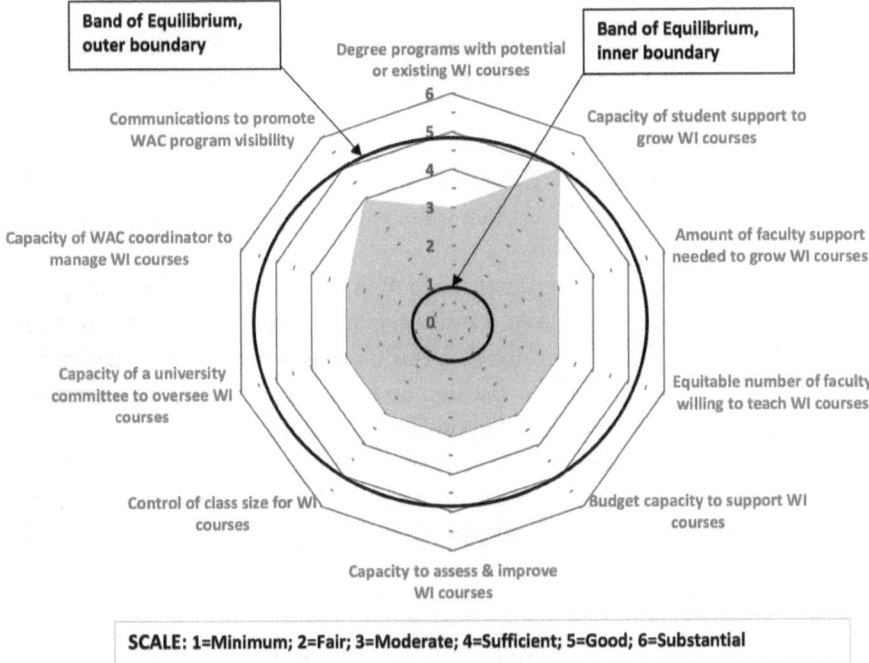

Figure 4. WAC during years of support from strategic initiative and revision of general education.

VI. History Lessons

Haswell (2001) writes that "programs are living, dynamic systems, whose parts have to differ to function," and not everyone will experience or understand them the same way. . . . This is the actual ecology, the essential synergy, the real history" of how WAC evolves (p. 2). The foregoing evaluation of one such program's dynamic systems, differing parts, and evolution suggests that history only means something if it successfully reveals "the integration of lived experience with the theoretical framework" that a whole-systems approach can afford (Walvoord, 2018, p. xi). Such an approach to an institution's history of WAC can enable its administrators and stakeholders to see where they can make "the kinds of sustainable and transformational changes that have long been the goal of the field"—and how they can counteract "the lack of resilience that has plagued so many WAC programs and may threaten the field itself" (p. 234).

Along these lines, what insights does this particular whole-systems approach to one institution's history of WAC reveal that other institutions might take into consideration? Possibly, the following:

- External consultant-evaluators such as those from the CWPA can play a critical role in establishing a precedent and local institutional context for assessing WAC-program sustainability.
- Serviceable SIs and institution-specific rubrics may derive from a combination of whole-systems theory and institutional criteria for assessing other programs or initiatives, when it's not feasible to collaborate more closely with WAC stakeholders.
- A whole-systems assessment of WAC's history can yield the long (and quantifiable) view of WAC's institutional impact on faculty and students.
- Historical patterns surface that can indicate what systemic factors have contributed to WAC's expansion and contraction—and the effects that these patterns have exerted upon faculty and students.
- Useful ways to deal with or work around obstructions to WAC's development and continuity become clearer with a whole-systems approach, as do the ways that campus ideologies about writing have evolved or devolved.

And, in general:

- A history of WAC, informed by whole-systems theory, can provide a powerful instrument for program advocacy

As for advocating for WAC at my university—or any other university—making and updating historical studies from a whole-systems approach can also provide a basis for keeping university-wide conversations about writing at the forefront. Such a history can thus bring stakeholders together at regular intervals for WAC pulse-checks. Such a history can raise questions and encourage stakeholders and decision-makers to focus on how WAC's SIs might change to accommodate demographic shifts in student populations, keep pace with enrollment concerns, reflect adjustments to admission requirements, affect retention rates, and so forth. And most important, such a history can inform a university about its faculty's desire to engage in the high-impact practices that uphold the quality of general education and undergraduate majors.

At the same time, several recommendations emerge from this historical study. WAC program administrators who would undertake a similar project should plan from the start to set up and maintain a close working relationship with the institution's writing center and join it in developing mutually useful data-gathering strategies. They should obtain annual reports and eight-year reviews of the UWC and

FYC programs to see where collaborative ventures have—or could have—benefitted them all. They need to form an immediate alliance with the university's professional development office to coordinate workshops and other events. They will also want to establish a rapport with university assessment officers and the university's annual data reporting centers to see how WAC assessment might be folded into these entities' routine operations. WAC administrators should identify the university's committees for curriculum development and improvement—and wherever possible, examine annual summaries of these committees' activities. Under advisement, they might embrace opportunities to serve in other administrative roles where WAC could feasibly participate in academic units' functions and policy-making efforts. They should network with key campus leaders whose institutional memory will help put WAC's mission and goals in perspective.

Twenty-some years is a daunting span of time to reconstruct WAC's presence on a university campus. But using whole-systems theory has helped me (and will help others) gain a much clearer picture of what the program has been, what it is, and what it can become. I surmise that if other WAC administrators on other campuses replicate a similar project, they can gain the same.

References

Association of American Colleges and Universities. (2010). Value rubric development project. https://www.aacu.org/value/rubrics.

Baccalaureate Review Task Force. (2009). *Discovering What NIU Graduates Should Know, Value, and Be Able to Do.* Northern Illinois University, 2009.

Banks-Wilkins, S., Recording Secretary. (2009). Minutes for the NIU Board of Trustees. Northern Illinois University. 1-10.

Brady, L. (2004). A case for writing program evaluation. *WPA: Writing Program Administration, 28*(1-2), 79-94.

Condon, W. & Rutz, C. (2012). A taxonomy of writing across the curriculum programs: Evolving to serve broader agendas. *College Composition and Communication, 64*(2), 357-382.

Cox, M., Galin, J.R., & Melzer, D. (2018). *Sustainable WAC: A whole systems approach to launching and developing writing across the curriculum programs.* NCTE.

Cox, M. & Galin, J. R. (2020). Tracking the sustainable development of WAC programs using sustainability indicators: Limitations and possibilities. *Across the Disciplines, 16*(4), 38-60. https://wac.colostate.edu/docs/atd/articles/cox_galin2019.pdf.

Council of Writing Program Administrators. WPA consultant-evaluator service for writing programs. http://www.wpacouncil.org/aws/CWPA/pt/sp/consulting-services.

Data Book. (2018). Northern Illinois University. https://www.niu.edu/effectiveness/_files/niu-data-book-2017-2018.pdf.

Haswell, R. H. (2001). Value-added studies: Defending the circle." In R. H. Haswell (Ed.), *Beyond outcomes: Assessment and instruction within a university writing program* (pp. 107-124). Ablex Publishing.

Inter/National Coalition for Electronic Portfolio Research. (2017). http://incepr.org/index.html.

McLeod, S. (1991). Requesting a consultant-evaluation visit. *WPA: Writing Program Administration, 14*(3), 73–77.

PLUS Task Force. (2014). Report to Provost. Northern Illinois University.

Thaiss, C., & Porter T. (Feb. 2010) The state of WAC/WID in 2010: Methods and results of the U.S. survey of the international WAC/WID mapping project. *College Composition and Communication, 61*(3), 534-570.

Walvoord, B. E. (1992). The future of WAC." *College English, 58*(1), 58-79.

Walvoord. (2018). Foreword. In Cox M., Galin, J.R., & Melzer, D. (Eds.), *Sustainable WAC: A whole systems approach to launching and developing writing across the curriculum programs* (pp. ix-xi). NCTE.

Designing for "More": Writing's Knowledge and Epistemologically Inclusive Teaching

LINDA ADLER-KASSNER

Drawing on data from alumni who have participated in a year-long faculty learning seminar, this article describes how working from writing's professional knowledge can facilitate faculty from other disciplines to create "more" epistemologically inclusive teaching.

Introduction

Writing professionals understand that the focus of our discipline—working with people to study writing—leads to conversations about teaching that extend well beyond writing per se. That's because writing is "never just writing" (Adler-Kassner). Instead, it is two things: the representation of knowledge-making in specific contexts, what we might think of as *writing as noun*, and a process that can be used to explore those contexts and practices, what we might think of as *writing as verb*. This latter perspective is reflected in Sandra Tarabochia's assertion that WAC/WID facilitators can and should act as "designers" with faculty colleagues outside of our discipline, understanding that we can facilitate "investigation[s] of the process of change as an experience of learning" (72). This investigation, Tarabochia asserts, involves collaborative activity that contributes to faculty members' understandings of their own and others' experiences with meaning-making within the specific context of their own disciplines, especially as they occur through writing. (72–73).

This article reports on a study of faculty participants in a seminar that is grounded in this notion of writing's professional knowledge. Labeled neither "WAC" nor "WID," the seminar is based on the idea that writing is never just writing but is instead a product (writing as noun) and a process (writing as verb) integrally related to epistemologies and identities. These include disciplinary epistemologies and identities in which faculty participate by virtue of their membership in academic disciplines. They also include the epistemologies and identities that students bring to those disciplines, especially introductory courses designed to introduce them *to* those disciplines. The analysis here comes from research that investigates the question: is the seminar "working"? The term *working* is shorthand for enactments of writing's professional knowledge: engaging faculty in the study of knowledge and knowledge-making practices in their disciplinary contexts, then working with them to take actions to make these practices more explicit, accessible, and inclusive. The presumption is that engaging faculty in examination of these epistemologies and identities is *sui generis*—it must accompany the development or refinement of writing or other teaching strategies intended to provide students opportunities for disciplinary participation, enactment of epistemologically inclusive teaching. This study (and ongoing work with faculty) suggest, then, that WAC and WID activity always necessarily extends well beyond writing.

The idea that writing's disciplinary knowledge can foster investigations of epistemologically inclusive teaching is reflected in a number of threshold concepts: "writing provides a representation of ideologies and identities" (Villanueva); "writing is linked to identity" (Scott); "writing is performative" (Lunsford); or "disciplinary and professional identities are constructed through writing" (Estrem). This idea also builds on related theories beyond writing described throughout this study. When these theories are put into dialogue with one another, they provide ways to understand knowledge-making as an exchange between: (1) the epistemologies and identities of learners, and (2) the contexts in which learning takes place—courses created by faculty members with their own epistemologies and identities who operate within disciplinary contexts. For a process of exchange between learner and faculty/contextual epistemologies to occur, faculty members *must* make the knowledge-making practices (epistemologies and their enactments) visible and accessible for students. Writing is a representation of those practices; hence, examining the practices in relation to writing is crucial.

Especially important for this approach to considerations of epistemologically inclusive teaching are two frameworks for learning. The first is "threshold concepts" (Meyer and Land), concepts that shape the ways members of disciplines perceive, interpret, and communicate their worlds. The second is "ways of thinking and practicing" (Hounsell and Anderson), context-specific moves learners make within contexts that are bounded by threshold concepts. As learners (including faculty) develop expertise through an immersive process that is reflected in successful learning in these disciplines, the constituent elements of their expertise become more tacit, more difficult to understand as things that are not "natural" or "commonsensical." These constituent elements include, but are not limited to, the threshold concepts that form the basis for action-taking within disciplines (e.g., what questions are asked and not asked, what evidence or data is understood as appropriate, what methods for analysis are preferred; and of course how learning is represented, for example, in writing). When learners do not have access concepts, though, they are not able to participate in either practices or ontologies associated with them—and when this occurs, they are often unsuccessful. Research has shown that the struggles of students who do not have this access, learners who are not what Joan Middendorf and David Pace refer to as "preeducated," can be especially pronounced among underrepresented, low income, and first-generation students (3), and especially in STEM disciplines (e.g., Reigle-Crumb et al). The seminar discussed here seeks to address these issues by enabling faculty to develop a foundation for epistemologically inclusive teaching, and then to develop teaching strategies from that foundation.

Study Site and Background

Faculty included in this study are alumni of a yearlong seminar funded by a Title V grant from the US Department of Education. Institutions designated "Hispanic Serving" are eligible to apply for the funding; UC Santa Barbara was designated an HSI in 2014, and is also an AANAPISI (Asian American, Native American, Pacific Islander Serving Institution). Our student population is diverse. Institutional demographics point to a few characteristics: 30 percent are Chicanx/Latinx, 27 percent are Asian-Pacific Islander, 44 percent are first generation college students, and 40 percent are Pell grant eligible.

The emphasis in this seminar, as in the grant itself, is on creating affordances for faculty to build on their knowledge as they teach our diverse student population. The seminar's goal is to enable faculty to develop a foundation for epistemologically inclusive teaching, and then to develop teaching strategies from that foundation. To achieve this goal faculty analyze disciplines, courses, and learning experiences—their own and their students'—through four knowledge domains, represented in figure 1.

The term *domain* draws on Peter Gärdenfors' research into semantics and geography to refer to a space structured to contain related concepts (5). At the same time that they conduct this analysis, faculty develop pedagogical strategies to enact epistemologically inclusive teaching, situating them within one or more of these domains. The domains, which are illustrated extensively later in this study, are these:

- Disciplinary knowledge: knowledge-making practices within disciplines, that is, disciplinary epistemologies as represented in threshold concepts (Meyer and Land) and the ways in which those epistemologies are enacted (e.g., "ways of thinking and practicing" [Hounsell and Anderson]).
- Representational knowledge: ways that knowledge-making is represented, typically in writing
- Empathetic knowledge: understanding others' identities and experiences; "forming and confirming" knowledge with others (Campelia)
- Learning knowledge: knowledge about how learning occurs—over time, with practice and feedback (e.g., Bransford et al; National Research Council).

Together, domains and teaching strategies constitute a "conceptual space," "a [correlated] collection of one or more domains" (Gärdenfors, 26).

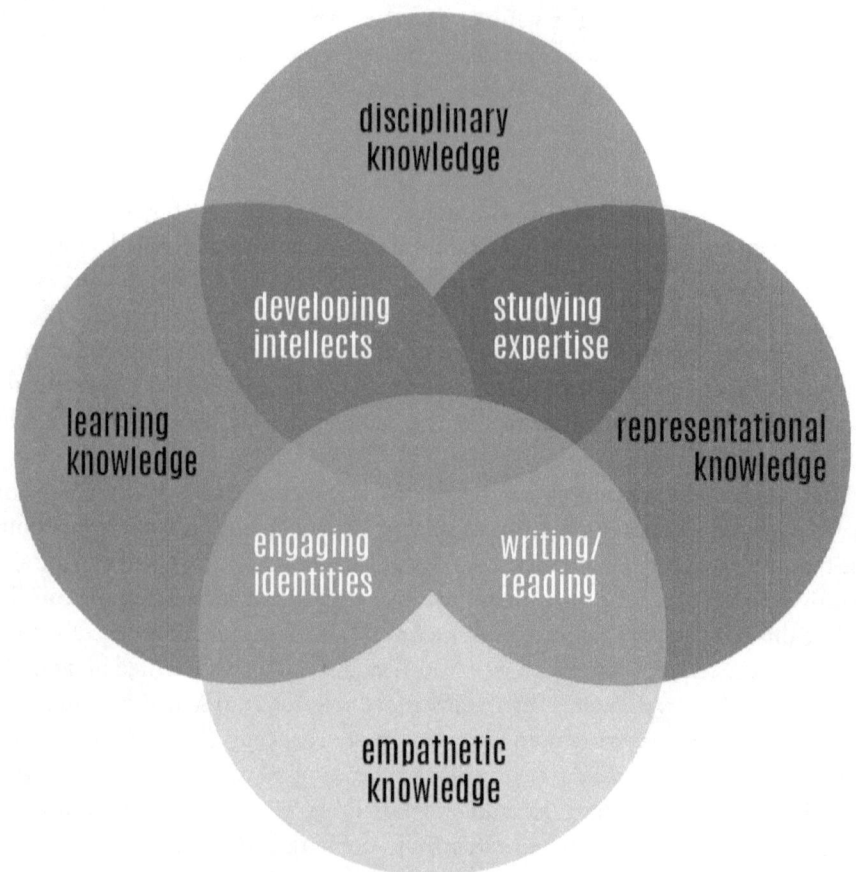

Figure 1: Knowledge domains and pedagogical activity model. Figure created by the author.[1]

---

1. This visual, made by my brilliant colleague Madeleine Sorapure, emerged from the analysis of this study, as well data from earlier studies (e.g., Adler-Kassner and Majewski; Wardle and Adler-Kassner). While I have always said that its goal (or outcome) was to foster epistemologically inclusive teaching, when the seminar began in 2015 I could not have represented the pathways to this goal in the ways I do in this description, nor in the visual. This representation has emerged in collaboration with faculty in the seminar. As I have sought to understand the seminar's effects (by interviewing and having focus groups with them), I also have shared the findings with them; they have helped to name some of these findings and distill them into visualizations like the one here.

What Working Means: "More" Epistemologically Inclusive Teaching

As above, the intent of this seminar is for faculty to structure pedagogical activities intended to facilitate learning through one or more of the knowledge domains outlined above, creating what Gärdenfors calls a correlated collection. The question that I sought to address in this study was whether the seminar was doing this, that is, whether and how faculty were designing pedagogical activities enacted through one or more domains. If they were doing so, the study then examined how that was occurring and where faculty saw the impacts—in their classes, with students, in departments, and/or beyond (i.e., to policies or approaches).

The data collected show how faculty are creating these collections by intentionally structuring teaching through the four domains: making disciplinary knowledge explicit and accessible, making expectations for composed knowledge (aka writing) visible and connecting those to disciplinary knowledge, enacting empathetic knowledge by creating structures to understand students' perspectives and experiences, and taking into account what we know about learning in the process of creating courses. The data also show that how faculty do this, that is, how they structure these activities through knowledge domains in order to create epistemologically inclusive teaching, depends on the faculty members and their individual disciplines.

Faculty members' efforts to create epistemologically inclusive teaching can be understood as falling into two broad categories. For some faculty, inclusive teaching means making these domains explicit so that students can more readily access the knowledge and associated practices of the disciplines. Extending recent work by Ann Pendelton-Jullian and John Seely Brown, I refer to this process as working "in the world," that is, helping students learn to create things *within* the structures of disciplines. Working "in the world" contains elements of WAC pioneer Barbara Walvoord's notion of "micro-level actions," collaborating with faculty individually or through their departments, "chang[ing] individual teacher behavior by persuasion" (62–63). For others, inclusive teaching means beginning to dismantle some of the structures of their discipline, analogous to Pendelton-Jullian and Seely Brown's idea of working "on the world." Here, they say, people design "structures and practices . . . that shap[e] contexts themselves through actions taken and things designed (Pendelton-Jullian and Brown, 162). Inclusive teaching as working "on the world" addresses issues that Walvoord labeled "macro"—questions about relationships between structures, like curriculum, and institutional cultures. This idea of inclusive teaching also resembles some of the activity called for by stage two WAC advocates like Mahala and Swilky and addresses concerns raised by Susan McLeod that as WAC was institutionalized it would become "homogeniz[ed]" or "bland," focusing on "merely" adding writing to existing courses rather than leveraging writing's role in teaching and learning to "bring about changes" (343).

As a person committed to epistemologically inclusive and socially just teaching, I of course have my own preferences for how I would *like* faculty in the seminar to approach their thinking about and actions associated with this teaching. At the same time (parallel to, part of, and sometimes in conflict with that preference), I recognize that disciplines have distinctive characteristics and ways of making meaning—and those associated with my/our discipline cannot take precedence over those of another's. However, I can draw on extant research into analyses of meaning-making within disciplines to better understand faculty members' approaches (an act that, in fact, contributes to my own development of empathetic knowledge). Researchers have long studied disciplinary epistemologies and meaning-making practices (e.g., Becher and Trowler; Donald; Poole). Becher and Trowler, for instance, provide four broad categories to situate these approaches:

- "hard-pure," disciplines like physics where knowledge is considered to be "cumulative, atomistic, concerned with universals, quantities, simplification"; knowledge is "impersonal and value free," and there is "clear consensus over significant questions to address";
- "soft-pure," disciplines like history where knowledge is "reiterative, holistic, concerned with particulars, qualities, complications, personal, and value-laden; where there are "disputes over criteria for knowledge verification ... and a lack of consensus over significant questions to address;
- "hard-applied," disciplines like mechanical engineering or medicine, where knowledge is "purposive, pragmatic, concerned with mastery of the physical environment, where criteria for judgment are purposive and functional"; and
- "soft-applied," disciplines like education or law, where knowledge is "functional, utilitarian, concerned with enhancement of practice, and often results in protocols or procedures (Becher and Trowler 36).

Especially at the level of introductory courses, the experience of faculty in our seminar who belong to disciplines that fall within the "hard-pure" or "hard-applied" category—generally those coming from STEM disciplines—have chosen to work "in the world," making their disciplinary practices more explicit. This is in part because they perceive a greater degree of consensus around what "knowledge" means and how it is explored and developed. I should note that the seminar includes a number of readings (e.g., Prescod-Weinstein; Dewsbury; Chamany; Tanner) that invite faculty to consider an alternative perspective, that disciplinary knowledge is personal and associated with values and ideologies of disciplines. Faculty within "soft-pure" and "soft applied" disciplines—generally humanities and social science disciplines—have sometimes (but not always) chosen work "on the world," exploring (and sometimes challenging) disciplinary knowledge. Here, too, the seminar includes invitations for faculty to realize that even as they are committed to inclusive practice, they are in positions of epistemological authority that requires them to establish some boundaries around knowledge-making practices, and that those boundaries are (by virtue of their appointments as successful faculty members at a research university) inflected by the disciplinary ideologies in which they have been inculcated and in which they participate (see Wardle and Adler-Kassner for an extensive discussion of the ideologies of disciplinarity, boundaries, and threshold concepts).

As for students, these ideas can be "troublesome" (Meyer and Land) for faculty; in keeping with stage 4 approaches to WAC and the reality that for faculty (as for students) change takes time and practice, readings are included as invitations for thought, not requirements for change. For this reason, I operationalize "working" as engaging in the four knowledge domains outlined here to *create greater epistemological access and opportunity for students within the context of faculty members' disciplines*—including their disciplinary (and personal) identities and practices—amidst the tensions of those disciplinary knowledge-making practices outlined above.

To study whether or how the seminar has enabled faculty members to create greater epistemological access within the context of their disciplines, graduate researcher Danny Katz and I facilitated two ripple effect mapping (REM) sessions (Chazdon et al.) for faculty who had participated during its first two years (2016–17 and 2017–18). REM provides a structure whereby evaluators design a loose framework for participants in change activities to discuss perceptions of "effects." However, beyond providing the discussion framework and attempting to record the debrief from discussions, evaluators do not engage in participants' discussions or debriefs. We provided faculty with a set of questions about (1) what they saw as takeaways from their participation and how and whether these connected to existing ideas; and (2) if they had takeaways, what they saw as effects from those takeaways, things that had happened to them, with students, to their teaching, etc. (Note that each path included a "no takeaways/no effects" option, i.e. faculty could say, "I had no takeaways/there have been no effects." [See appendix A for REM protocols given to faculty.])

Faculty began by conducting "appreciative inquiry interviews" with each other in groups of two or three. These are interviews designed to elicit rich descriptions of experience through discussion. Following the appreciative inquiry interviews, teams create ripple effect maps, visual heuristics that they could use to structure an analysis of the rich descriptions they provided in conversation with each other. In our sessions, we described to the assembled groups the process and visual heuristic that we imagined for these maps. Danny [who served as the primary facilitator] provided more detail about the REM process, explaining that we had derived five possible categories for "effects" based on our analysis of previous REM efforts:

- No effect: the seminar didn't do anything for you
- Small effect (local, isolated, etc.): the seminar only had an effect on you, and maybe you haven't enacted it in your class (but you intend to)
- Medium effect (local, community, etc.): you enacted something you learned from the seminar in a class you teach and it influenced others as well
- Large effect (department, policy, etc.): you enacted something you learned in the seminar and it's spread to other faculty, your department, or overarching ways of thinking
- Unexpected effect: the seminar had some effect that doesn't work with this linearized version of the ripple effect. Had some distal effect or unexpected effect.

Danny told participants that if these sorting structures didn't work for them, they were free to use any that seemed more appropriate.

Following team mapping, groups looked across the maps and tried to create an all-session map. Each of our two REM sessions included two groups. The two groups in the first session reviewed one another's maps; the two groups in the second session were able to look across the maps of groups from the previous session and their own. While there were differences in placement of some "effects" across the groups (i.e., some labeled effects as "small" while others called them "medium"), there was consistency in discussion of effects across all of the groups and their maps. These consistencies were indicated in individual group maps and the collective maps created by the four teams in group discussion after the appreciative inquiry interviews.

Ten seminar alumni (of the twenty-four who were part of the first two years) participated in REM sessions held in December 2018. All but one (Bruce) were teaching classes that enrolled between 90–300 students. The majority of the evidence in this analysis comes from those faculty. The REM participants include:

Bruce - graduate program in environmental science. Bruce was the only faculty member teaching courses with fewer than 90 students in the study group.

Mary - Psychological and Brain Science. Mary's focus in the seminar was a research methods course.

John L. - Ecology, Evolutionary, and Marine Biology (EEMB). John's focus was on two courses, biology of infectious disease and biology of non-infectious disease.

Drew- Probability and Statistics. Drew was focusing on the first required statistics course students take after declaring their majors.

Samantha (a pseudonym) - teaching a large course in her department that fulfilled the university's "writing requirement" (analogous to a WI requirement).

Walid – Communication. Walid was focusing on a social marketing course.

John H. – Economics. John H. was focusing on an intermediate macroeconomics course.

Three other faculty participated in this study; the recording device for their discussion failed so their voices are included only in analysis of the large-group discussion (which was recorded by several other devices):

Vanessa – Psychological and Brain Science. Vanessa was also focusing on a research methods course.

Kathy – Molecular, Cellular, and Developmental Biology. Kathy was focusing on an intermediate biology course.

Morgan – Chemistry. Morgan was focusing on organic chemistry lab courses.

To provide additional illustrations of the points raised by REM participants, the descriptions below also include data from in-depth individual interviews conducted in June–July 2016 with faculty who participated in the first year of the seminar. These participants include Kate, a faculty member in History; Rolf, a faculty member in molecular biology; and Dolly, a faculty member in communication. REM transcripts, as well as earlier data from faculty interviews, show how faculty perceive the seminar to be "working," that is, leading them to create what they consider to be epistemologically inclusive teaching through the domains of disciplinary knowledge, representational knowledge, empathetic knowledge, and learning knowledge. To illustrate, I next define each domain in greater detail and provide excerpts from faculty interviews to show them in action.

Domain 1: Disciplinary Knowledge

Disciplinary knowledge refers to knowledge-making practices within disciplines—disciplinary epistemologies and the ways in which those epistemologies are enacted. In the seminar, I ask faculty to access these epistemologies through thinking about threshold concepts (Meyer and Land) and ways of thinking and practicing (Hounsell and Anderson). Briefly, threshold concepts are concepts through which learners in any discipline must think to be successful. Ray Meyer and J.F. Land, the researchers who initially identified threshold concepts, describe several attributes associated with learners' experiences with them. They are *liminal*—learners' progress toward them takes a one-step-forward-two-steps-back trajectory toward and away from passing through the "threshold" of a threshold concept. They can be *troublesome*, as they challenge learners' existing understandings and ways of operating for a number of reasons (Perkins 2006). They can be *transformative*—they change the ways learners think and understand. They also are *integrative*, as once learners "see" or think through threshold concepts, they affect their understandings beyond the immediate context. They are likely *irreversible*—it's hard to revert to earlier ways of seeing. Finally, they are associated with *expert practice* (Bransford et al)—experts see through and with threshold concepts as a series of patterns, where novices do not.

As experts in a research university, "disciplinary knowledge" is central to faculty members' identities; they are here *because* their disciplinary knowledge has been recognized and validated through processes associated with those disciplines as "communities of practice" (Lave and Wenger). They have earned advanced degrees, their research and/or teaching is regularly reviewed and validated by colleagues, and so on. Faculty are also deeply interested in and motivated by disciplinary knowledge, even when or if they seek to broaden its boundaries, as I note above in the discussion of working "on the world." Intellectually, this knowledge is part of their "academic home" (Poole), where they are comfortable and have deep understandings of how to function. The seminar also asks faculty to focus on undergraduate courses *in* faculty members' disciplines, courses that are by definition intended to introduce students to fundamental precepts and ways of operating in those disciplines.

But in many of these courses, some learners—especially underrepresented and low-income learners—are less successful than others. This is especially true in STEM disciplines; on our campus it is also the case in some social science disciplines. Extending from research in writing studies (e.g., McCarthy, Carroll; Beaufort) and building on extensive work in other disciplines (e.g., Bransford et al.; Chamany; Tanner), the seminar begins by asking participants to engage with *theoretical knowledge* about epistemologies of disciplines articulated by examining threshold concepts (Meyer and Land) and/or ways of thinking and practicing (Hounsell and Anderson), and *practical/experiential* knowledge about teaching and learning in disciplines.

Discussing "takeaways" from the seminar, faculty in the REM sessions described a number of features associated with disciplinary knowledge as they defined threshold concepts or ways of thinking and practicing. Faculty also returned to these elements of disciplinary knowledge in their discussions about "effects" of the seminar. Walid (communication) described a threshold concept in the social marketing class that he was focusing on in the seminar: "[the] concept of reciprocity . . . that we work on everything communally" and people are not bringing expertise to collaborators.

Mary (psychology and brain science) named "what a hypothesis is" as central to the disciplinary knowledge that was foundational for her research methods course. John L. (EEMB) didn't name specific disciplinary concepts, but did discuss the importance of identifying these concepts for students: "if they learn nothing else," he said, "then they should learn the threshold concepts because that'll allow them to move to a new level, perhaps." In in-depth interviews, year 1 participants (not part of the REM study) also named other elements of disciplinary knowledge that they considered to be critical for successful learning: using the "scientific approach" to study communication (Dolly, communication), participating in science as a researcher "designing experiments that answer questions with unknown outcomes" (Rolf, molecular biology), "analyz[ing] why and how certain historical, social, political narratives speak to particular audiences in particular times and places" (Kate, history). The domain of disciplinary knowledge is perhaps most accessible to faculty because it is closest to their everyday lives in the academy; at the same time, that closeness makes outlining its boundaries all the more important and, sometimes, challenging.

Domain 2: Representational Knowledge

Where disciplinary knowledge is perhaps most familiar to seminar participants, representational knowledge is the domain most likely to feel familiar to those in writing studies. It extends directly from the expertise of writing: "how learning is represented," that is, through writing or other forms of composed knowledge. This idea is perhaps the central organizing principle of WID research, which studies "the writing that occur[s] in disciplinary classes" (Bazerman, et al., 10). It is reflected in threshold concepts of writing studies: writing is a way of enacting disciplinarity (Lerner); disciplinary and professional identities are constructed through writing (Estrem); genres are enacted by writers and readers (Hart-Davidson). When faculty from other disciplines express concerns about student writing to writing instructors or program directors, their concerns are often about representational knowledge, the idea that students "can't write" or are struggling to write appropriately in their courses or disciplines. In the seminar, faculty worked through theoretical knowledge about how learning is represented in writing, as well as practical/experiential knowledge of writing as part of the learning process (both their own and their students').

REM session participants described a number of takeaways associated with representational knowledge. Samantha, a faculty member teaching a writing intensive course in her department, said that she was "trying to think through the diverse learning environment or skills environment, and thinking about learning in that way." Her "main concern" was "design[ing] assignments that were clear, that were not asking [students] to do too much." John (EEMB) said that "I realize[ed] that just being able to write with a new set of terminology, or being able to speak with a new set of terminology, is difficult for students." This realization, he said, "made me think more about the way I grade exams . . . in terms of even a short answer question. If it's worded oddly does that mean the student doesn't understand it, or does it mean they're learning to use this new terminology?" Drew, from statistics, followed John's comment, saying that he now gives students examples of "what I want the write up to look like." By considering the role(s) that writing plays in students' learning within their classes and disciplines, faculty come to understand representational knowledge as a practice that is integrally related to other domains, rather than a stand-alone or separate activity.

Domain 3: Empathetic Knowledge

"Empathetic knowledge" is developed as faculty consider how learners represent themselves and their identities *in* learning. Historically, empathetic knowledge has been used as a shorthand to refer to degrees of enactment of two kinds of empathy: cognitive, that is, the ability to understand the perspective of another, and affective: "the experience of emotion, elicited by an emotional stimulus" (e.g., Cuff et al 147; Pendelton-Jullian and Brown 148). More recently, though, researchers like medical ethicist Georgina Campelia have redefined empathetic knowledge as a *reciprocal practice*: something that is co-constructed as people—in this case, faculty and students—seek to learn about one another's perspectives, identities, and experiences while simultaneously considering our own. Enacting empathetic knowledge as a practice, faculty members' roles are to look for moments of intersection and divergence among identities and experiences, attempting to "form and confirm knowledge with others" (Campanella 530)—rather than just trying to find ways for others to approach their disciplinary knowledge, or understand how people are doing so. When I shared this model with faculty participants, they also felt it important to add metacognition to this domain, since that implied reflexive awareness of one's own actions in relation to perceptions of others' positions, responses, and actions.

Especially in the domain of empathetic knowledge, too, the literature on racial stereotyping and racism (e.g., Steele; Yosso et al.; Milem et al.), the learning experiences of underrepresented learners (Mallinson and Charity Hudley; Charity Hudley, et al.), and the construction of disciplinary knowledge practices as they relate to race (Chamany; Prescod-Weinstein) are central. Depending on their experiences as learners and their disciplines, faculty have greater and lesser degrees of experience with this focus, and I find it crucial in the seminar to make room for multiple ways of thinking about and acting on these ideas. Thus, seminar participants read peer-reviewed literature on issues associated with identities and learning, as well as pieces published in more mainstream publications (including some written by academics, e.g., Coates; Nadworny; Jack). Additionally, faculty conduct interviews with one of their former students—preferably those who didn't do very well in their course. With the student's permission, these interviews are transcribed and become an additional set of readings for discussion.

In group discussions following appreciative inquiry interviews, both seminar alumni groups placed empathetic knowledge centrally in their maps. Faculty indicated that they understood more about students and their experiences, a manifestation of empathetic concern; understood how those experiences were different from their [the faculty members'] own; and thought about these as they structured their courses. For instance, faculty reflected on how they reflected on their own experiences as learners and how this reflection affected their thinking about teaching. Walid (communication) realized that coming from a highly educated family,

> the thing that I definitely want to take away is the extent to . . . [I come into class with] assumptions. . . . [L]earning came very easy to me and I knew the tricks. I don't know how it came to me but I knew the tricks and I knew how to study. I knew how to plan how long to take on each exam. I had these tricks in place. And it was a good reminder that, and I sort of assume that to be the case for everyone, which is definitely not the case, especially for first generation.

John L. (EEMB) also thought the differences between his experiences and that of his students. Reflecting on the availability of information for students, John L. said, "it's easier for them, but in some ways it's harder, I realize. And I hadn't really—I'm, I knew this. It was something I knew but hadn't addressed, hadn't really had a chance to think about with people." Bruce, a faculty member in ecology, referred to the importance of "understanding at a deeper level the diversity of student backgrounds and the consequential differences in what they're bringing to the table." Mary (psychology and brain science) described realizing that it was helpful for her to share her own experience with students, sharing with them "how I came [to be a faculty member] and how my parents didn't go to college so I was a first generation student." Mary, for instance, said that "One thing I really got out of it was the idea of how students are just going from class to class. . . . They're required to think or how they're supposed to approach problems or . . . reading or . . . anything . . . assignments in different classes are just so different." Mary, Walid, and John H. (economics) also described the effects of increased empathy: "We all talked about how we ended up with more empathy for our students. So that's kind of local to us and then [we talked about] various ways that we changed . . . how we taught the class. . . ." Concurring with a comment about having "more empathy" for the students in the group discussion, for instance, Samantha said, "I didn't go in thinking that would happen, but that's exactly happened . . . I had more empathy because I knew more about them."

Domain 4: Learning Knowledge

Learning knowledge refers to considerations of processes associated with learning. Several principles from the research underpin this portion of our work. First is the idea that experts are able to understand the study of their subject within disciplinary boundaries. These boundaries are rooted in threshold concepts (Meyer and Land 2006). When novice learners encounter these concepts, though, they must undergo a process of learning about them. This process can be troublesome for a variety of reasons, for example, it can bump up against existing ideas or challenge inert knowledge or ways of understanding the world (Perkins). Once experts perceive subjects through threshold concepts, they are better able to undertake learning in the contexts where those concepts are situated because they better understand what kinds of questions to ask (and not ask), how to interpret evidence or data, and how interpretation is represented [generally in writing]. The ability to perceive these expectations also facilitates learners' abilities to make conceptual connections between different ideas, producing "critical thinking" or "analysis" that serve as the hallmark of learning. Another important element in this domain is time—that is, the time it takes to approach, engage in, and manifest learning. The time element is especially important given that UCSB is on ten-week quarters.

Study participants described this knowledge through the reading and through their experience *as* learners in the seminar, often blending the two together in their responses. John L. said "It was really interesting for me to see how students might come into my class from a social science background and have difficult using the terminology . . . not because they're poor speakers or poor writers. It's just because it's new to them." Drew, John L's interview partner, immediately agreed: "we . . . talked a lot about . . . the idea that students don't inherently come into your course knowing how to navigate your course."

Consistent with the last part of John L. and Drew's comments, participants also described their understandings of learning knowledge through course concepts. Economist John H. discussed his evolving understanding of the learning bottlenecks that were faced by students in his high-stakes intermediate macroeconomics course. "They just view solving [economic] problems as mathematical process and have no idea what the mathematical steps mean. Whereas, I go through these problems . . . I know what these processes mean. So, I have to be cognizant of that . . . I can't take it for granted when I talk to a student that when I say I'm taking a derivative that they really know what a derivative means conceptually and not just mathematically." And participants discussed their evolving understandings of students' movement between classes through understandings of learning knowledge. As these comments indicate, faculty participants' understandings of learning knowledge are deeply rooted in disciplinary knowledge and representational knowledge, as well.

Epistemologically Inclusive Teaching: Pedagogical Activity as Intentional Action Through Knowledge Domains

"Epistemologically inclusive teaching," as I describe above, is defined here as teaching that makes explicit knowledge-making practices (epistemologies and their enactments) visible and accessible to students and provides students the opportunity to engage with those practices. For some faculty, this means making practices more explicit so that students can see and participate in them more readily ("working in the world"); for others, it means making practices more explicit so that students [and faculty] can interrogate and change them ("working on the world"). The pedagogical activities that faculty develop in their courses—from structuring a curriculum, to designing assignments, to providing materials via lecture or discussion, to assessing student work—are manifestations of epistemologically inclusive teaching practices, the enactment of how faculty seek to create "more" inclusive spaces in their courses and enable learning that works in the world or on the world.

The REM sessions demonstrated how faculty developed and implemented epistemologically inclusive teaching practices, locating them as intentional actions that were situated within one or more of the four knowledge domains (disciplinary, representational, empathetic, learning). This emphasis on intentional action that is connected to a domain is critical, as it counters the idea that "good teaching" or "active learning" can be achieved through the use of tips and tricks, that is, the kinds of strategies that are sometimes highlighted distinct from context on commercial websites, or reflected in requests to writing faculty members for course assistance, for example, whether we can offer one-off workshops on things like "commenting on student writing." But creating a division between the other domains and writing-teaching-learning activities has long been a central concern among WAC faculty (e.g., Walvoord; McLeod 1989; Mahala and Swilky). To illustrate how faculty enacted epistemologically inclusive teaching in their disciplinary contexts, then, I next draw on transcripts of REM sessions to illustrate this idea in action. Prior to each transcript excerpt, I indicate the knowledge domain(s) with which the faculty members' comments are associated.

John L. and Drew: Working in the World

> John L. (EEMB) and Drew (statistics) provide a compelling illustration of faculty connecting pedagogical activity through the four knowledge domains in order for students to work *in* the world. This means that John and Drew are creating more accessible ways for students to access the knowledge of their disciplines through teaching practices. In this excerpt, they are describing their takeaways from the ONDAS seminar.

John L.:

Empathetic: I think the main takeaway I got from it was what it is like to be a learner again

Learning: so it was really interesting for me to see how students might come into my class from a social science background and have difficulty using the terminology for example, (Representational/Disciplinary) not because they're poor speakers or poor writers. (Learning) Not because they're poor speakers or writers, but It's just because it's new to them.

Drew:

Learning/Disciplinary/Pedagogical activity: Something I took away from the beginning . . . was . . . thinking about what are the hurdles or the pieces of the course that are going to trip up students and trying to be conscious about explaining those.

Learning/Disciplinary: I also we thought talked a lot about . . . the idea that students don't inherently come into your course knowing how to navigate your course . . . that was a big part of thinking about how what my expectations were for the students . . . that the students didn't know what those were, that they . . . maybe didn't understand those things.

John L:

Learning/Disciplinary/Empathetic: I love having these non-STEM majors in my [general education] classes, but I hadn't really thought too much about how difficult it is for them . . . [N]ot just this aspect of different expectations and different writing expectations in different subjects . . . I realize that just being able to write with a new set of terminologies, or being able to speak with a new set of terminology, is difficult for the students.

Pedagogical activity: It's really made me think more about the way that I grade exams . . . in terms of even a short answer question, if it's worded oddly does that mean the student doesn't understand it, or does it mean they're struggling to use this new terminology?

Drew:

Pedagogical activity: In terms of thinking about my teaching, this wasn't the direction I was thinking about my teaching. I was thinking more about using tools I could use. Oh, I've got to put some stuff up online and I've got to put interactive exercises and things like that. . . . [But] there's a bunch of things that I do differently now. . . . I certainly structure my syllabus at the beginning where

I highlight, okay, these are the three threshold concepts in this course, without saying that literally to them, but I sort of say these are the three sort of key ideas that we're working towards in this course. . . .

Representational: I'm very conscious now when I'm giving assignments of having more guidance as to how I want them completed. For instance, we do data analysis labs and I give them an example of what I want the writeup to look like.

In this exchange, John L. and Drew are connecting pedagogical activity through the other domains associated with pedagogical expertise, expressing those ideas in ways that demonstrate their application to teaching students to work "in the world." Both are talking through the domains identified here to design teaching that helps students more easily access and work with ideas associated with their classes and disciplines that they consider important. Figures 2 and 3 provide a visual representation of small portions of their discussion. In each, elements of their dialogue are plotted in the vicinity of the domain with which they are most associated. The pedagogical activity that these considerations connect to is located in the center of the diagram.

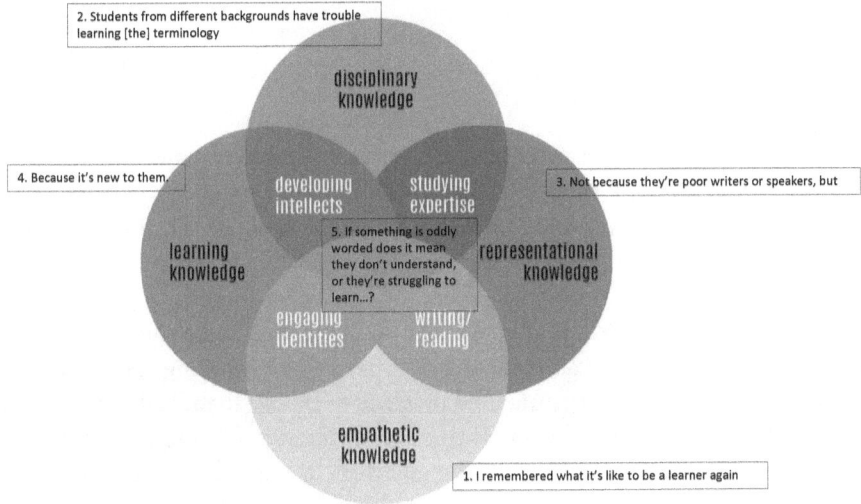

Figure 2. "In the world": Partial representation of John L.'s enactment across pedagogical domains. Figure created by the author.

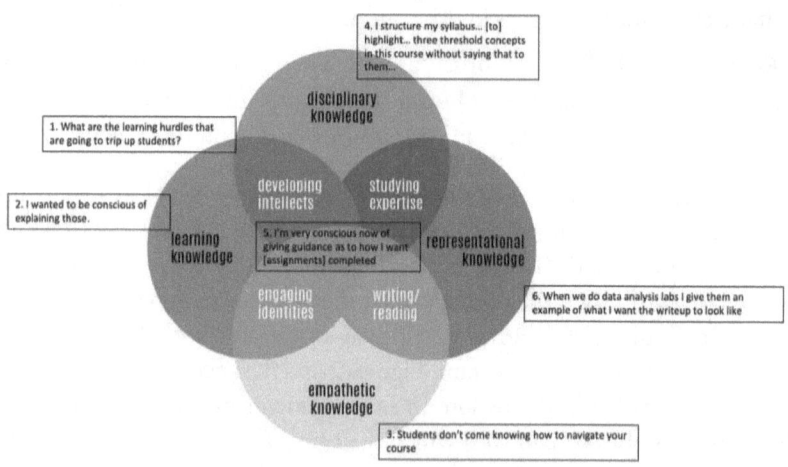

Figure 3. "In the world": Partial representation of Drew's enactment across pedagogical domains. Figure created by the author.

Walid: Working on the World

John L. and Drew's excerpts demonstrate how faculty described effects that here are associated with the idea of more accessible practices to enable students to work "in the world," creating more accessible pathways for students to access the disciplinary and representational knowledge of the discipline through faculty members' own understandings of empathetic knowledge, learning knowledge, and pedagogical practice. Excerpts from Walid's descriptions of takeaways from the faculty seminar demonstrate how these pathways can come together to illustrate working "on the world." This involves working on structures and practices to change them and to potentially change the contexts where design takes place. To show this sense of "working," I again break Walid's contributions into sections that correspond with each of the four domains: disciplinary knowledge, representational knowledge, empathetic knowledge, and learning knowledge. I also note the intentional connection to pedagogical practice included in the contributions. Figure 4 illustrates correspondences with the model outlined here.

> *Disciplinary:* So the biggest takeaway . . . I sort of landed on this concept of reciprocity with communities . . . the idea . . . that we work on everything communally and I'm not bringing my expertise to them. . . .

Pedagogical practice: And literally as we were talking about this idea about our communities we're working with I said what would it look like if I fully applied that ethic to this class?

Representational: And I had them write and turn in stuff.

Empathetic: My TA read [what they handed in] and said [students seemed to be complaining]. But I tried to pause and say . . . let's really honor them, which is what I was trying to do. . . .

Pedagogical: [As a result of taking their feedback seriously], I changed the syllabus organization. I changed the number of assignments. I changed the type of assignments. I changed about a third of the things that I did . . . I really sort of pushed the idea of honoring students as a community myself, and how well I was doing that or not as part of this class. . . .

Walid's description of the effects of his takeaways—redesigning multiple elements of his course, including the ways in which students could provide input into that design—provides an illustration of how he created more opportunities for students to expand the epistemological boundaries of the class extending from the threshold concept that he identified.

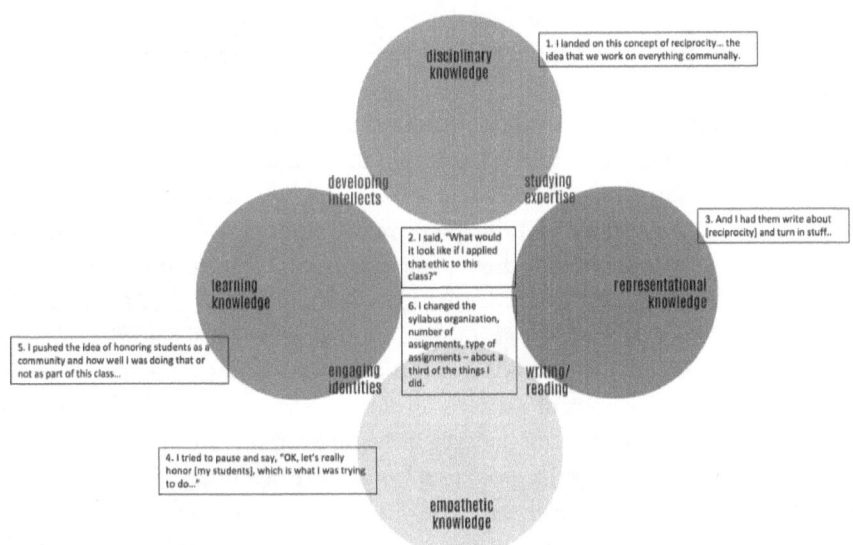

Figure 4. "On the world": Partial representation of Walid's enactment across knowledge domains

Writing's Knowledge and Faculty Learning

The model that I've used to describe these "more" inclusive practices—focusing faculty learning within and across domains—has gradually emerged from the three years of this seminar, as well as from data collected from seminar participants in this study and a previous one (Adler-Kassner). Conceptually, it draws heavily on work by threshold concepts researchers and others who have focused on faculty learning through conceptual frameworks (e.g., Meyer; Timmermans; Entwhistle; Irvine and Charmichael; Bunnell and Bernstein; Wardle), as well as on research to understand faculty change (e.g. Martensson et al). Part of this effort has also involved creating ways for faculty to act on the integral connections between each of these domains, especially as they connect to pedagogical practice. The model also has been influenced by the necessity to connect these domains to practical strategies that faculty can use in their teaching. The challenge here, as for when faculty ask writing teachers for "quick tips" (e.g., "can you do a forty-five-minute workshop on commenting on student writing?") is this connection between conceptual theory and actual practice. As in the case of the "forty-five-minute workshop on quick tips," teaching activities must be intentionally connected (conceptually and in operation) by faculty to and through the other domains here— disciplinary knowledge, representational knowledge, empathetic knowledge, and learning knowledge,. Otherwise, the chance of understanding what they are intended to do, much less whether or not they are achieving their effect, which is to say "working," is virtually impossible to understand or assess.

The emphasis on intentionality and the location of teaching activities within specific domains is closely affiliated with pedagogical expertise outside of writing studies, as well. Based on an extensive review of the literature, for instance, Elvira et al. provide ten "instructional principles" framed through a theory of pedagogical expertise. They place these into three large categories: "Transforming Theoretical/Conceptual Knowledge into Experiential/Practical Knowledge" (192), "Explicating Procedural/Experiential Knowledge into Conceptual/Theoretical Knowledge" (195), and "Reflecting on . . . Practical and Conceptual Knowledge by Using Self-Regulative Knowledge" (196). Elvira et al.'s categories can be seen as a parallel framing of the idea proposed here, that epistemologically inclusive teaching involves situating activities within the four knowledge domains I outline: disciplinary, representational, empathetic, and learning. Similarly, Novak et al, whose work on concept mapping represents an attempt to provide structural practices to link learning behaviors and processes, contend that learners (in this case, faculty learners) must have a "*conceptual* understanding of the phenomenon they are investigating" for activities to contribute to their "relevant knowledge" (p. 4).

Ian Kinchin has built on the foundation laid by Novak et al. to explore expert learning (and teaching). Advancing an argument that itself reflects extensive research on novice-expert practices (e.g., Bransford), Kinchin then identifies a paradoxical challenge if these domains are not integrated into teaching practice. Experts, he says, are able to both connect discrete ideas in linear patterns, creating "chains" of practice, and to connect those chains to other chains in meaningful and hierarchical ways that are situated within contexts, creating what he calls "nets of meaning" (2–3). But often, when teachers create lessons for students, "the[ir] complex (often hierarchical) understanding . . . is converted to a linear . . . sequence of lecturers and tutorials. From this the student is expected to construct [his or her] own understanding of the topic. The students' understanding is then assessed using a linear format (such as an essay or a multiple choice paper). In such scenarios the hierarchical structures held by student and teacher remain private whil[e] only the linear translation is shared for scrutiny" (4–5).

Consistent with the idea of employing writing's professional knowledge to facilitate learning, then, data from this study, distilled into the knowledge domain model outlined here, illustrates how writing professionals can create ways for faculty to explore disciplinary, representational, empathetic, and learning knowledge and then to apply that learning to their teaching. For the model I have outlined here, the literature associated with the development of expertise, especially work by I. M. Kinchen and references in that work to concept mapping have been especially important. The argument advanced in these texts, that the construction of hierarchical maps that are joined together through expressions of intentional practice, has been generative for me and as I put the ideas embedded in it into practice, for faculty. This occurs as faculty learn within each domain and, in some instances, map their understandings along different dimensions—"geometrical structures" (Gärdenfoers 6) that help to guide the application of participants' understandings and ideas—within each domain. For instance, within the domain of "disciplinary knowledge" are concepts associated with articulating epistemologies and ontologies of disciplines (such as "community of practice," "threshold concepts," and "ways of thinking and practicing"). The vertical dimension in this domain, "disciplinarity," locates "disciplinary concepts" at the top and "subdisciplinary concepts" at the bottom. The horizontal axis, "level of learner," locates "novices" at the left end and "experts" at the right. Figure 5 is a heuristic I use often with faculty to think about these dimensions, asking them to focus their thinking or locate their ideas within its boundaries.

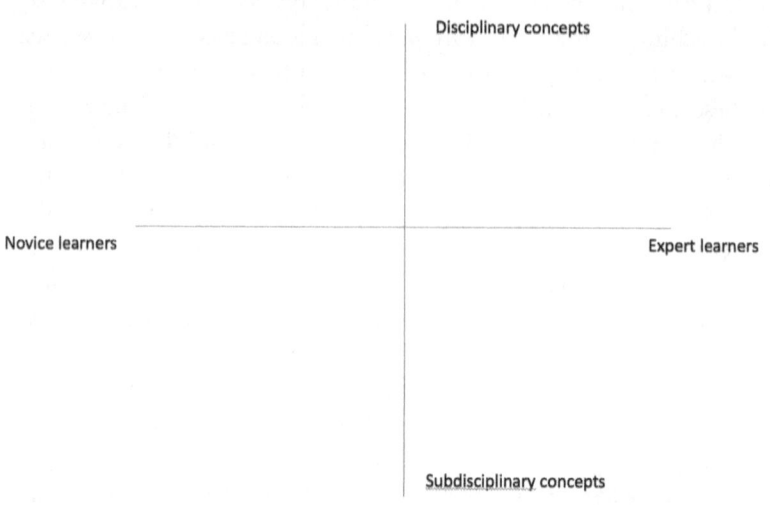

Figure 5. Disciplinary concept/learner heuristic. Figure created by the author.

While separating faculty members' reflections into domains (and dimensions within each domain) may seem to pull apart activities and conceptualizations that are integrally related, the very act of pulling them apart, like layers of an orange, seem to enable faculty to understand and then to reconstruct/redesign their teaching into a different whole. From the perspective that writing is composed knowledge that is grounded in epistemologies, identities, cultures, contexts, beliefs, and practices, then, people who are *in* writing—that is, writing studies professionals—can work with others to think about writing from this perspective, too. That is: we can work with others to move understandings of writing from questions of the practical (what kinds of assignments can I create? How can I give effective feedback?) to questions about composed knowledge (what does good learning and writing look like here?) and processes of composing (can I use writing to better understand? To help students better understand?). As this study shows, faculty find that participating in a seminar that extends this perspective affects their teaching in multiple ways. As the analysis of the transcripts through conceptualizations of expertise suggests, it also seems to contribute to the development of teaching expertise that is manifest in more epistemologically inclusive teaching practices.

Acknowledgment

Thank you to Madeleine Sorapure for (yet again) creating brilliant visuals to illustrate my thinking. Thanks, too, to *WAC Journal* reviewers who provided valuable feedback on the initial submission of this article.

Works Cited

Adler-Kassner, Linda. "CCCC Chair's Address: Because Writing is Never Just Writing." *College Composition and Communication*, vol. 69, no. 2, 2017, pp. 317–40.

—. "Rethinking Epistemologically Inclusive Teaching." *(Re)Considering What We Know: Learning Thresholds in Writing, Composition, Rhetoric, and Literacy*, edited by Linda Adler-Kassner and Elizabeth Wardle, UP of Colorado/Utah State UP, 2019.

Bazerman, Charles, et al. *Reference Guide to Writing Across the Curriculum*. Parlor Press, 2005.

Becher, Tony, and Paul R. Trowler. *Academic Tribes and Territories: Intellectual Enquiry and the Culture of Disciplines*. 4th ed., The Society for Research into Higher Education and Open University Press, 2001.

Beaufort, Anne. *College Writing and Beyond: A New Framework for University Writing Instruction*. Utah State UP, 2007.

Bransford, John, et al. *How People Learn: Brain, Mind, Experience, and School*. National Academy Press, 2001.

Bunnell, Sarah, and Daniel Bernstein. "Overcoming Some Threshold Concepts in Scholarly Teaching." *Journal of Faculty Development*, vol. 26, no. 3, 2012, pp. 14–18.

Campelia, Georgina. 2017. "Empathetic Knowledge: The Import of Empathy's Social Epistemology." *Social Epistemology* vol. 31, no. 6, 2017, pp. 530–44.

Carroll, LeeAnn. *Rehearsing New Roles: How College Students Develop as Writers*. Southern Illinois UP/NCTE, 2002.

Chamany, Kayatoun. "Science and Social Justice." *Journal of College Science Teaching*, vol. 36, no. 2, 2006, pp. 54–59.

Charity Hudley, Anne, et al. *The Indispensable Guide to Undergraduate Research*. Teachers College Press, 2017.

Chazdon, Scott, et al., editors. *A Field Guide to Ripple Effects Mapping*. University of Minnesota Libraries Publishing, 2017, conservancy.umn.edu/handle/11299/190639

Coats, Ta-Nahisi. "Acting French." *The Atlantic*, August 2014. www.theatlantic.com/education/archive/2014/08/acting-french/375743/. Accessed August 2019.

Cuff, Benjamin, et al. "Empathy: A Review of the Concept." *Emotion Review*, vol. 8, no, 2, 2016, pp. 144–13.

Donald. Janet. *Learning to Think: Disciplinary Perspectives*. Jossey-Bass, 2002.

Elvira, Quincy, et al. "Designing Education for Professional Expertise Development." *Scandinavian Journal of Educational Research*, vol. 61, no. 2, 2017, pp 187–204.

Entwhistle, Noel. "Threshold Concepts and Transformative Ways of Thinking Within Research into Higher Education." *Threshold Concepts within the Disciplines*, edited by Ray Land, Jan H.F. Meyer, and Jan Smith. Sense Publishers, pp. 21–36, 2008

Estrem, Heidi. "Disciplinary and Professional Identities are Constructed Through Writing." *Naming What We Know: Threshold Concepts of Writing Studies*, edited by Linda Adler-Kassner and Elizabeth Wardle. Utah State UP, 2015, pp. 55–57.

Gärdenfors, Peter. *Conceptual Spaces: The Geometry of Thought*. MIT Press, 2000.

Hart-Davidson, Bill. "Genres are Enacted by Readers and Writers. *Naming What We Know: Threshold Concepts of Writing Studies*, edited by Linda Adler-Kassner and Elizabeth Wardle. Utah State UP, 2015, pp. 39–40.

Hounsell, Dai and Anderson, Charles. "Ways of Thinking and Practicing in Biology and History: Disciplinary Aspects of Teaching and Learning Environments." *The University and Its Disciplines: Teaching and Learning Within and Beyond Disciplinary Boundaries*, edited by Carolin Kreber. Routledge, 2009, pp. 71–83.

Irvine, Naomi and Patrick Carmichael. "Threshold Concepts: A Point of Focus for Practitioner Research." *Active Learning in Higher Education*, vol. 10, no. 2009, pp. 103–119.

Jablonski, Jeff. *Academic Writing Consulting and WAC: Methods and Models for Guiding Cross-Curricular Literacy Work*. Hampton, 2006.

Jack, Abraham Anthony. "I was a Low-Income College Student. Classes Weren't the Hard Part." *New York Times Magazine*, September 10, 2019. www.nytimes.com/interactive/2019/09/10/magazine/college-inequality.html. Accessed September 13, 2019.

Kinchin, Ian. *Visualising Powerful Knowledge to Develop the Expert Student: A Knowledge Structures Perspective on Teaching and Learning at University*. Sense Publishers, 2016.

Lerner, Neal. "Writing is a Way of Enacting Disciplinarity." *Naming What We Know: Threshold Concepts of Writing Studies*, edited by Linda Adler-Kassner and Elizabeth Wardle. Utah State UP, 2015, pp. 40–42.

Lunsford, Andrea. "Writing is Performative." *Naming What We Know: Threshold Concepts of Writing Studies*, edited by Linda Adler-Kassner and Elizabeth Wardle. Utah State UP, 2015, pp. 43–44.

Mahala, Daniel, and Swilky, Jod. "Resistance and Reform: The Functions of Expertise in Writing Across the Curriculum." *Language and Learning Across the Disciplines*, vol. 1, no. 2, 1994, pp. 35–62.

Mallinson, Christine, and Anne Charity Hudley. "Partnering Through Science: Developing Linguistic Insight to Address Educational Inequality for Culturally and Linguistically Diverse Students in U.S. STEM Education." *Language and Linguistics Compass*, vol. 8, no. 1, 2014, pp. 11–23.

Martinson, Katarina, et al. 2011. "Developing a Quality Culture through the Scholarship of Teaching and Learning." *Higher Education Research and Development*, vol. 30, no. 1, 2011, pp. 51–62.

McCarthy, Lucille, and Fishman, Steven. "Boundary Conversations: Conflicting Ways of Knowing in Philosophy and Interdisciplinary Research." *Research in the Teaching of English*, vol. 25, no. 4, 1991, pp. 419–68.

McCarthy, Lucille. "A Stranger in Strange Lands: A College Student Writing Across the Curriculum." *Research in the Teaching of English*, vol. 21, no. 3, 1987, pp. 233–65.

McLeod, Susan. "The Future of WAC— Plenary Address, Ninth International Writing Across the Curriculum Conference, May 2008 (Austin, TX)." *Across the Disciplines*, vol. 5, 2008, pp. 1–6.

Meyer, Jan H.F. "Variation in Student Learning as a Threshold Concept." *Journal of Faculty Development*, vol. 26, no. 3, 2012, pp. 9–13.

Middendorf, Joan, and Pace, David. "Decoding the Disciplines: A Model for Helping Students Learn Disciplinary Ways of Thinking." *New Directions for Teaching and Learning* 98, 2004, pp. 1–12.

Milem, Jeff, et al. *Making Diversity Work on Campus: A Research-Based Perpective*. Association of American Colleges and Universities, 2012.

Nadworny, Elissa. "'Going to Office Hours is Terrifying' and Other Tales of Rural College Students." National Public Radio, 12 December 2018. www.npr.org/2018/12/12/668530699/-going-to-office-hours-is-terrifying-and-other-hurdles-for-rural-students-in-col. Accessed 29 September 2019.

Novak, Joseph, and Cañas, A.J. *The Theory Underlying Concept Maps and How to Construct and Use Them*. Technical Report IHMC Cmap Tools. Institute for Human and Machine Cognition, 2008.

Pendelton-Jullian, Ann, and John Seely Brown. *Design Unbound: Designing for Emergency in a White Water World*. MIT Press, 2018.

Perkins, David. "Threshold Concepts and Troublesome Knowledge." *Overcoming Barriers to Student Understanding*, edited by J.F. Meyer and Ray Land. Routledge 2006, pp. 33–47.

Poole, Gary. Academic Disciplines: "Homes or Barricades?" *The University and Its Disciplines: Teaching and Learning Within and Beyond Disciplinary Boundaries*, edited by Carolin Kreber. Routledge, 2009, pp. 50–57.

Prescod-Weinstein, Chanda. medium.com/@chanda

Riegle-Crumb, Catherine et al. 2019. "Does STEM Stand Out? Examining Racial/Ethnic Gaps Across Postsecondary Fields." *Educational Researcher*, vol. 48, no. 3, 2019, pp. 133–44.

Scott, Tony. "Writing Enacts and Creates Identities and Ideologies." *Naming What We Know: Threshold Concepts of Writing Studies*, edited by Linda Adler-Kassner and Elizabeth Wardle. Utah State UP, 2015, pp. 48–50.

Steele, Claude. "A Threat in the Air: How Stereotypes Shape Intellectual Identity and Performance." *American Psychologist*, vol. 52, no. 6, 1997, pp. 613–29.

Tanner, Kimberly. "Structure Matters: Twenty-Once Teaching Strategies to Promote Student Engagement and Cultivate Classroom Equity." *CBE-Life Sciences Education* vol. 12, 2013, pp. 322–31.

Tarabochia, Sandra. *Reframing the Relational: A Pedagogical Ethic for Cross-Curricular Literacy Work*. National Council of Teachers of English, 2017.

Timmermans, Julie. "Identifying Threshold Concepts in the Careers of Educational Developers." *International Journal for Academic Development*, vol. 19, no. 4, 2014, pp. 305–17.

Villanueva, Victor. "Writing Provides a Representation of Ideologies and Identities." *Naming What We Know: Threshold Concepts of Writing Studies*, edited by Linda Adler-Kassner and Elizabeth Wardle. Utah State UP, 2015, pp. 57–59.

Walvoord, Barbara. 1996. "The Future of WAC." *College English*, vol. 58, no. 1, 1996, pp. 58–79.

Wardle, Elizabeth. "Using a Threshold Concepts Framework to Facilitate an Expertise-Based WAC Model for Faculty Development." *(Re)Considering What We Know: Learning Thresholds in Writing, Composition, Rhetoric, and Literacy*, edited by Linda Adler-Kassner and Elizabeth Wardle. UP of Colorado/Utah State UP, forthcoming, 2019.

Wardle, Elizabeth, et al. "Recognizing the Limits of Threshold Concepts Theory: Boundedness and Liminality." *(Re)Considering What We Know: Learning Thresholds in Writing, Composition, Rhetoric, and Literacy*, edited by Linda Adler-Kassner and Elizabeth Wardle. UP of Colorado/Utah State UP, forthcoming, 2019.

Wiseman, Theresa. "A Concept Analysis of Empathy." *Journal of Advanced Nursing*, vol. 23, 1995, pp. 1162–67.

Yosso, Tara et al. "Critical Race Theory, Racial Microaggressions, and Campus Racial Climate for Latina/o Undergraduates." *Harvard Educational Review*, vol. 79, no. 4, pp. 659–90.

Appendix A: REM protocol

Faculty questions

Stage 1: Inquiry interviews (~30 minutes, participants interview each other)

1. Your name, name you'd like to be referred to for this research (if not your name), and your discipline?

Part 1: Reflection

1. What do you see as takeaways, if any, from the ONDAS seminar?
    a. If you didn't have any takeaways, why do you think you didn't?
    b. If you did: did these takeaways connect to existing ideas that you had?
        i. If so, what were those and what were the connections?
        ii. If not, what was new about them, and why did they strike you as potentially useful?

Part 2: Implementation

1. If you have had takeaways:
    a. Have these takeaways had effects for you? Please be as specific as possible: class approaches, assignments, activities, or something that you've thought about since participating in the seminar. Can you make connections from your takeaways to these specifics?
2. If you haven't had takeaways: what do you think prohibited or prevented you from taking things away from the seminar?

Part 3: Effects

1. If you have had takeaways:
    a. What do you think has happened – to you, with students, to your teaching – connected to your takeaways? Please be as specific as possible – focus on a person, class day, or something else if you can.
        i. What of these effects did you expect? What didn't you expect?
    b. If you would like to: is there a student you think demonstrated especially impressive work to demonstrate these effects? What did the student do?

Stage 2: Mapping

The following text was provided in a brief (10 minute) slide presentation:

Slide 1: Goals

- Simple: Trying to figure out what's happening by mapping, metaphorically, how the program has influenced your actions as faculty/instructors, locally and otherwise.
- The metaphor is imagining a pebble thrown into a pond:
    - Bluntly, the pebble represents the ONDAS seminar. Has it had an effect on the pond?
    - The effect of the pebble extends outwards, with local effects as well as unexpected effects via ripples

Slide 2: Consider three levels of effects

- No Effect: The ONDAS Seminar didn't do anything for you
- Small effect (local, isolated, etc): ONDAS only had an effect on you, and you maybe haven't even enacted it in your class (but intend to).
- Medium Effect (local, community, etc): Enacted something you learned from ONDAS in a class you teach and it influenced others as well
- Large Effect: Enacted something you learned in ONDAS and it's spread to other faculty, your department, overarching ways of thinking
- Unexpected Effect: Some Effect that doesn't work with this linearized version of the ripple effect. Had some distal effect, unexpected effect

Slide 3: possible REM model

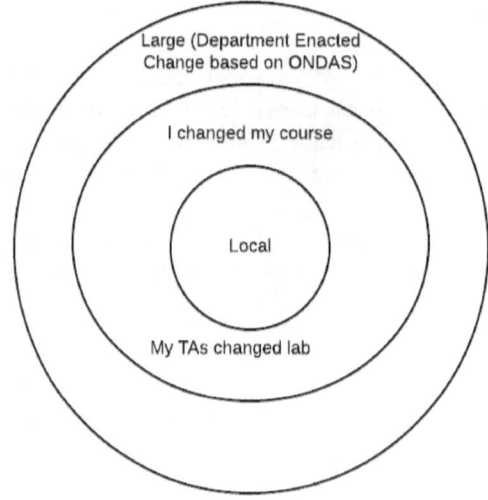

Slide 4: Examples (from Chazdon et al)

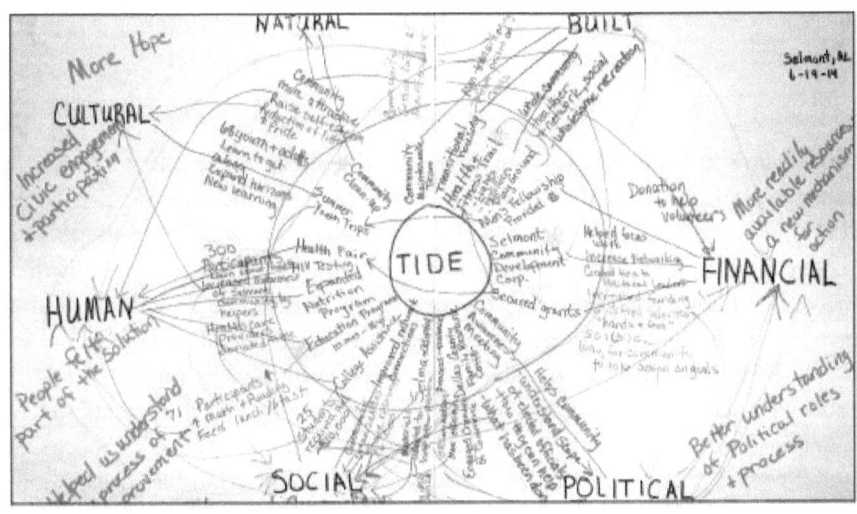

Writing's Knowledge and Epistemologically Inclusive Teaching

Threading Competencies in Writing Courses for More Effective Transfer

AMY D. WILLIAMS AND JONATHAN BALZOTTI

This article contributes to current conversations about transfer, specifically how WAC courses can encourage vertical transfer (Melzer). The authors draw on research in learner development that demonstrates how a threaded curriculum approach helps students learn concepts and skills and apply that knowledge in multiple contexts. Additionally, a threaded curriculum can incorporate pedagogical elements that have been linked to effective transfer, such as abstract conceptualization and metacognition. The authors present an instructional model for sequenced writing courses that leverages this research and moves away from disconnected writing courses. The threaded curriculum explored here promotes vertical transfer between an introductory professional writing course and a professional writing internship course. Both classes explicitly thread common competencies (which the authors define as purposeful combinations of concepts, skills, and learning dispositions) and common pedagogical activities (experiential learning and reflection) throughout the curriculum. Though designed for professional writing courses, this threaded-competencies curriculum offers a pattern that can be adapted for WAC courses in any discipline.

Introduction

Transfer—how students use (or don't use) the knowledge and skills they learn in class in new contexts—dominates current conversations in all academic disciplines, including writing studies (Beaufort, Moore, Nowacek, Wardle, Yancey, et al.). Yet, Dan Melzer notes that much of the transfer literature focuses on what "individual instructors can do to encourage transfer" in a "lateral" way—particularly from first-year composition to other college courses (76). This focus may have resulted in less attention being paid to how knowledge transfers "vertically" as students progress to more advanced writing situations both in the university and the workplace. To encourage a more cohesive and comprehensive conversation, Melzer proposes the idea of a *vertical transfer writing curriculum* that encourages transfer both laterally (between first-year writing and other courses) and vertically (between increasingly advanced writing contexts). He reports his institution's efforts to create such a curriculum through several programmatic changes, including allowing students to fulfill their writing-intensive course requirement by taking a series of classes within their major.

Melzer offers few details of how departments might design these course series, but as teachers of professional writing we find his idea provocative. We believe faculty can work together to help students transfer knowledge and skills "vertically" to more advanced writing situations in both the university and the workplace. While we have conceptualized our collaborative framework in terms of writing across the curriculum, it is relevant to all teaching-and-learning enterprises across campus.

We see the problems of both lateral and vertical transfer in many of our students who are acquiring a particular set of communication skills and working toward professionalization. Even as these students develop writing knowledge and skill, they approach new writing courses and contexts with trepidation, unsure of their ability to succeed with unfamiliar and often more complex writing tasks. In part, their apprehension seems to arise from past experiences of being "batted back and forth between . . . noncommunicating assumptions and views" about writing as they have moved between classes (Graff 28). Unfortunately, we found that this "volleyball effect" occurs even within a Professional Writing and Rhetoric minor offered through the English department at our university. Our students, who come from a variety of majors, are required to take several writing courses within the minor. But even after completing these courses, students sometimes report finding it difficult to recognize how their knowledge and skills might transfer "up" as they move to what feel like riskier writing situations such as advanced courses within the minor and professional writing situations. To address this problem, we created a course sequence that aligns with Melzer's principles for vertical transfer writing. This paper describes our coordinated course sequence and the process we used to create a cohesive curriculum and pedagogy. Although we teach this curriculum in an English department, it can be adapted for sequenced writing courses in any discipline.

We accept that time spent developing writing skills in multiple courses certainly plays a valuable and needed role in preparing students for new writing contexts and tasks. However, we also agree with Melzer that lateral and vertical transfer are more likely to happen if the curriculum intentionally incorporates elements that support transfer. These elements include instruction in abstract concepts, multiple and varied opportunities to apply those concepts in different contexts, prompting that explicitly cues transfer of abstract concepts, and metacognitive activities that ask students to reflect on the reciprocal relationship between their abstract learning and concrete experiences (National). Our course design incorporates these elements by creating two curricular strands. The first strand is a reformulation of the idea of competencies, which we define as a combination of conceptual knowledge, skills, and learning dispositions. The second strand is a pedagogical approach that emphasizes experiential learning and reflection. We weave these two strands or "threads" through our two-course sequence. Threading competencies and an experience-reflection based pedagogy through a sequence of writing courses, we argue, can help students transfer knowledge across "lateral" and "vertical" writing contexts. Again, we describe courses in professional writing, but a threaded-competency curriculum is appropriate for courses across the curriculum.

Threaded Curricula

We borrow the concept of a threaded curriculum from K–12 educators, who developed the model to address concerns about traditional teaching models that overemphasize discrete subjects. These curricula can feel fragmented to students and disconnected from educational theories like multiple intelligences. A threaded curriculum promises a more unified learning experience by establishing "big ideas" that guide teaching and learning across academic subjects (Fogarty 63). In a K–12 context, these big ideas often focus on processes of learning: for example, thinking skills (e.g., prediction or analysis); social skills (e.g., collaboration or listening); or study skills (e.g., critical reading or reflection). These skills, or threads, form a "metacurriculum" for a number of courses—in some ways taking precedence over the unique subject matter of individual classes—which acts as a "vehicle for [the big idea] skills to be learned" (Kysilka 200). For example, at a particular grade level, teachers might establish a thread of information literacy—finding, interpreting, and evaluating information. Math, science, language arts, music, physical education, and even elective classes would then foreground information literacy, giving students opportunities to practice evaluating data with different disciplinary content. In K–12 contexts, threaded curricula appear both at the grade-level and within departments. Threaded models show students that knowledge and skills have lateral relevance (across classes at the same grade level) and, when implemented in succeeding grade levels, vertical relevance as well (in more advanced classes).

Though less common, threaded curricula also appear at the university level. For example, academic departments often link courses around their discipline's "big ideas" or "threshold concepts"—the foundational knowledge, principles, and vocabulary that students need to master as they progress toward expertise within that discipline (Meyer and Land). The literature includes examples of "big ideas" threaded curricula being used in diverse fields—from chemistry (Barth and Bucholtz) to nursing (Lewis et al.) to computer animation (Cumbie-Jones). Additionally, some universities use campus-wide threaded curricula by offering courses in multiple disciplines, all focused on a common theme. The theme acts as a "thread" that students explore through a variety of disciplinary perspectives. During the 2018–2019 academic year, for example, the University of Chicago offered courses clustered around thematic threads such as inequality, urban design, and history of the law, with classes taught in the humanities and social, physical, and biological sciences.

Of course, the most familiar application of a threaded curriculum at the university level is writing across the curriculum (WAC), where writing represents the "thread" for classes across campus (Fogarty and Stoehr). Though the thread of writing skill in WAC seems obvious, even WAC courses can feel disconnected for students when teachers narrowly focus on disciplinary writing conventions or idiosyncratic concepts rather than more universal writing skills, theory, and practice. If students do not recognize the broad threads that tie courses together, the WAC model may be less successful at promoting vertical transfer (Melzer). By presenting new knowledge in the context of already familiar concepts, teachers cue students to recognize opportunities for transfer (Perkins and Salomon). For example, students who learn a broad social action theory of genre are better prepared to analyze and understand the specific features of a new genre (Devitt "Genre Pedagogies"). Not all instruction needs to be connected across courses. Nevertheless, when making curricular decisions, teachers might ask themselves, "How could this skill, concept, or practice be threaded into another course?"

Our approach to sequenced writing instruction reflects the influence of both university-level and K–12 "threading" practices. Like the WAC model, we created threads that focus on writing skills, and like course clusters we emphasized conceptual knowledge that students explore across different contexts. From K–12 models, we adopted the notion of "big ideas" that represent ways of thinking or learning dispositions. We combined these elements—skills, conceptual knowledge, and learning dispositions—into what we refer to in this paper as competencies. Our skill-knowledge-disposition competencies are explicitly woven across two of our professional writing courses. The competency-based threaded approach of these courses helps students acquire specific skills, understand the theory that informs those skills, and develop dispositions for learning and thinking that lead to the successful application of skills and knowledge in diverse situations. Pedagogically, our courses use a model that draws on repeated cycles of instruction, concrete application and practice, and reflection (Kolb). The experiential-reflective cycle is the second "thread" of our curriculum.

This paper explains how we created and taught a two-course sequence using the threads of common competencies and an experience-and-reflection pedagogy. We call our combination of common competencies and pedagogy a *threaded-competency curriculum*. We suggest that a threaded-competency curriculum—organized around deliberate and transparent sequencing of course content, competencies, and opportunities for concrete practice and reflection—provides a more coherent and transferable learning experience for students. We also believe that teachers benefit from the dialogue that creating such a curriculum requires. The conversations we had while designing these courses forced us to do things we had sometimes neglected. For example, we had to honestly assess what we think students are able to do after taking our individual classes. While our department publishes learning outcomes for all courses, we realized that we hadn't always considered how the enactment of our individual curricula emphasizes and interprets those outcomes differently. Working as partners on a threaded-competency curriculum required us to be more mindful about what students actually learn in our individual classes. We also had to accept more accountability for how students apply and adapt knowledge from our classes in new academic and non-classroom contexts. Thinking of ourselves as answerable to each other and to our students for how our teaching transfers (not just how students' learning transfers) motivated us to imagine our work relationally—as partnerships with each other, other faculty on campus, and off-campus entities like employers. Having redesigned our courses with a conscious concern for threading competencies, we believe that this approach can be implemented in both writing and non-writing courses across campus.

Competency Threads

The competencies we created for our threaded courses are significantly different than our previous learning outcomes and came to replace those outcomes on our syllabi. In the past, our course learning outcomes were often descriptions of discrete knowledge or skills we hoped our students would acquire. In contrast, our new competencies reflect our desire to show students that professional writing skills are rooted in theoretical knowledge. We also wanted our competencies to acknowledge that successful writers share particular dispositions toward communication (Council). The competencies, then, represent a deliberate articulation (in both senses of that word) of the skills, theoretical knowledge, and learning dispositions students can develop over the two-course sequence. We thus see the competencies as elaborated learning outcomes, or what we might call meta-outcomes.

To determine competencies for our courses, we first identified the professional skills and knowledge we hoped students would acquire by the end of this two-course sequence (Wiggins and McTighe). Writing these down on sticky notes, we arranged the notes into affinity clusters, groups that included relatable skills and abilities needed to succeed in a wide variety of vocational endeavors. Not to be confused with narrow job-training, what we are calling affinity clusters are both practical and devoted to the larger goals we as instructors associate with a liberal education. Our competencies are also inspired by those David Guest articulated in his article "The

Hunt for the Renaissance Man of Computing," an early description of competencies that effective problem solvers and leaders in business possess (von Oetinger). We adapted some of Guest's competencies to better reflect our definition of competency as encompassing skills, conceptual knowledge, and dispositions relevant to writing. Finally, we aligned our competencies with the professional writing discipline and our department's goals for our courses.

Again, our three-part definition of competencies is a core component of our threaded curriculum. We teach our threaded courses in sequence, with Introduction to Professional Writing (IPW) offered fall semester and Advanced Professional Writing-Internship (APW) offered for the winter semester. Both courses use the following competencies:

- Collaboration
- Rhetorical Awareness
- Genre Literacy
- Ethics in Professional Communication
- Leadership

Table 1 shows the relationship between skill, theory, and disposition that forms the framework for each competency. Both courses weave these competency "threads" through the class readings, assignments, and experiential learning activities. Because the competencies remain consistent across courses, students have extended opportunities to develop and practice them. In essence, we used the competencies as the foundation of a curriculum that not only makes skills, concepts, and learning dispositions explicit but also gives students opportunities to practice their knowledge and skills in a variety of contexts, and that supports metacognition, with competencies providing students language for reflecting on how skills and knowledge can be reused, repackaged, and repurposed in more advanced writing tasks (Fogarty and Stoehr).

Table 1:

Competency principles mapped to theory, skills, and dispositions.

Competency	Theory	Skills	Dispositions
Collaboration	A sociocultural perspective of learning recognizes that individuals build understanding, skills, and group identification as they develop proficiency with others (Gee; Shaffer)	Work together to solve problems, create and share content, integrate research and share insights to develop a solution Receive and respond to feedback as group members innovate and venture new ideas to solve communication problems	The willingness to accept **responsibility** for one's actions and interactions with others The willingness to be **flexible** in working with others to accomplish tasks The willingness to be **open** to other ways of thinking and to **engage** with other people and their ideas to accomplish a common goal
Rhetorical Awareness	Rhetoric involves rhetors, audiences, and exigencies (Bitzer) Rhetors create exigencies by selecting and interpreting elements of the situation (Vatz) Rhetoric is an art of topoi that can respond to all situations while being sensitive to the particularities of each (Consigny)	Identify the rhetorical elements of a writing task—rhetor, audience, exigence Analyze the exigence as a selection and interpretation of the context Design a response that is appropriate to the particularities of a specific situation	The willingness to be **curious** about situations in the world The **flexibility** to adapt to different situations, expectations, or demands, to approach writing assignments in multiple ways The willingness to **reflect** on and be **responsible** for one's rhetorical choices
Genre literacy	Genres respond to recurring social situations (Devitt "Generalizing") Genre is social action (Miller) Genre is a reflection of discourse community norms, epistemologies, ideologies, and social ontologies (Berkenkotter and Huckin)	Identify the social situations to which genres respond Describe textual features as a response to a social situation and evaluate the flexibility of those features Describe the social action the genre accomplishes and experiment with generic responses to specific situations	The desire to be **curious** about generic forms and social situations and to use new methods to investigate questions, topics, and ideas The ability to **reflect** on one's own thinking and the individual and cultural processes that structure knowledge The ability to be **creative and flexible** in adapting genres for specific situations, expectations, and demands

Ethics in Professional Communication	Professional communicators follow ethical principles (Society) Ethics guide decision making (Markel) Ethics includes rhetorical strategies writers use (Duffy)	Critically examine examples of professional communication from various ethical perspectives Evaluate the competing demands professional writers face to produce useful, effective, and ethical communication Evaluate one's own writing choices as ethical decisions	The willingness to be **accountable** to others, to take **responsibility** for one's actions and the consequences of those actions The willingness to be **metacognitve** about the ethical beliefs and perspectives that motivate one's decisions
Leadership	Leadership is a process of influencing others (Taylor) Elements of leadership include forming a shared vision, aligning resources to accomplish that vision, and working to build commitment to that vision (Northhouse)	Create a shared vision to address a client's needs Develop strategies for idea structuring and goal setting (Mumford) Align resources to accomplish the shared vision Build commitment among the group	The desire to be **open** to others by listening and reflecting on their ideas and responses The ability to **create** a supportive communicative climate The willingness to accept **responsibility** for engaging and incorporating the ideas of group members to develop a shared vision for the project

* Some elements of our theoretical foundation are adaptations of Vetter and Nunes's course design.

Experiential Learning and Reflection Thread

In addition to our competency threads, we also integrated a pedagogical model that provides students opportunities to practice these competencies in multiple contexts and situations. These writing situations incorporate elements researchers have associated with successful transfer—active experimentation and reflection—through the interplay between theoretical knowledge and the demands of realistic and complex situations. By combining explicit competencies with an experience-and-reflection focused pedagogy, we better prepare students to transfer knowledge and skills between classrooms and workplaces.

We used David Kolb's model to create a pedagogy that asks students to recursively conceptualize, apply and practice, and reflect on their knowledge, skills, and writing experiences. Our threaded-competency pedagogy focuses on what Kolb describes as "grasping" and "transforming" experience through intentional and thoughtful practice and reflection. The Kolb learning model gave us a common pedagogical process for helping students develop and apply our agreed upon competencies both in and outside of our classrooms through four different activities (as shown in Figure 1) that encourage successful learning and transfer: experience, reflective observation, abstract conceptualization, and active experimentation (30). Central to the Kolb model is the learner's ability to connect abstract theoretical knowledge (in our case professional competencies) to concrete experiences through observation and reflection and to experiment with that knowledge in a range of situations. Learning occurs through a recursive process of applying knowledge and conceptual understanding to real-world problems and using real-world experience to modify conceptual knowledge. Kolb's definition of learning as "the process whereby knowledge is created through the transformation of experience" expresses our vision of students learning as they participate in a series of conceptually unified but increasingly complex and risky writing tasks (38).

This focus on sequenced experiential learning moves away from our earlier transmittal model of learning, where students learned ideas in the IPW classroom using traditional classroom assignments before moving to the internship experience in the APW course. Our new threaded curriculum emphasizes practicing competencies through experiential activity in both courses, helping students see a connection between the assignments in the introductory writing course and the more advanced internship course. Our pedagogical design recursively moves students between learning writing concepts, practicing writing tasks, and reflecting on their writing experiences. The recursive nature of the pedagogy helps students contextualize, decontextualize, and recontextualize their knowledge and skills to see their applicability to new situations, a process Perkins and Salomon call "high road transfer" (22). Research shows that students are more likely to transfer their knowledge when instruction connects skills to theoretical concepts, when teachers and students explore how those concepts and skills are relevant (or not) across different situations, when students have opportunities to apply concepts and skills in multiple and contrasting contexts, and when students monitor and reflect on their own learning experiences (National; Engle, et al.).

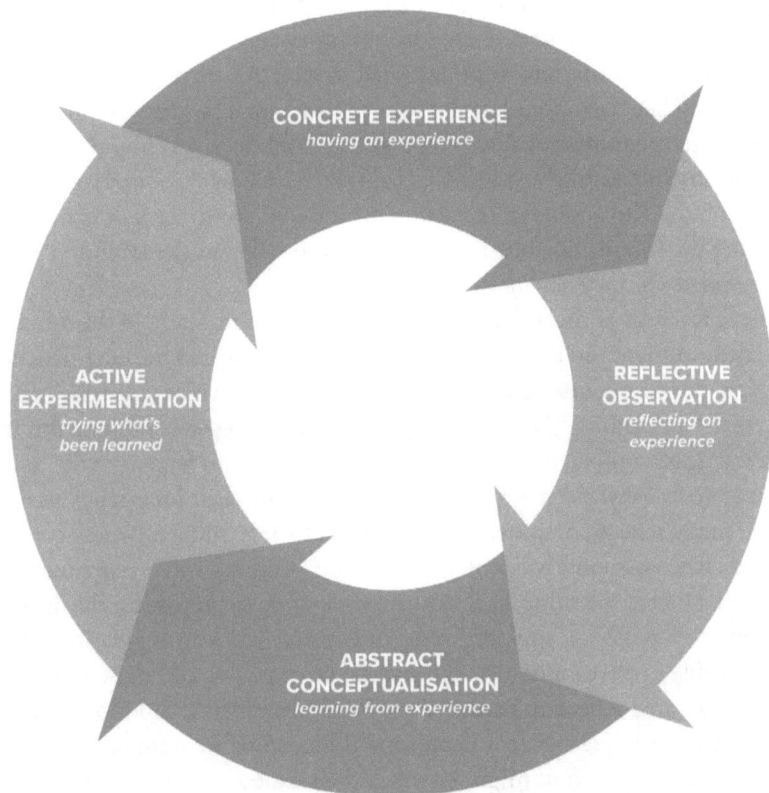

Figure 1. Kolb's Experiential Learning Model

Active experimentation gives students multiple opportunities to apply and test competencies they develop in our courses. There are three primary benefits to active experimentation: (1) students begin to refine the abstract ideas they formulated during the conceptualization stage of learning; (2) students strengthen their ability to think in abstract terms about experiences; and (3) students intentionally practice competencies.

Sequencing Writing Courses

Both the introductory professional writing course (IPW) and the advanced professional writing internship course (APW) are part of a minor in professional writing and rhetoric housed in the English department of the large private university in which we teach. The minor introduces students to rhetorical history, theory, and criticism as a foundation for composing effective texts in a wide variety of contexts and genres. Students are required to take a fundamentals of rhetoric class, a writing style class, and four other courses chosen from history and study of rhetoric, visual rhetoric, digital communication, or professional writing. As instructors, we saw that our students often failed to appreciate the theoretical ties that bind our minor's foundational classes to the professional writing courses. While students found rhetorical theory and history interesting, we needed to help them see how those ideas integrated up the curriculum. This problem, combined with our students' lack of confidence when entering the internship course, motivated us to redesign the IPW and APW around a threaded-competency model.

We believe teachers of threaded courses should spend time early in the semester helping students understand this unique approach to teaching and learning. Teachers should explain how the course readings, assignments, and activities represent a pedagogical process for acquiring the competencies. In our courses, we combine this initial introduction to competencies with reflection—asking students to write about their learning goals for the semester and more specifically their long-range writing goals. In this initial reflection, students imagine what their learning experiences (both in and outside the classroom) will look like, how their learning will prepare them for a profession that includes writing, and what they might do to prepare for the upcoming assignments. We also ask students to detail any previous learning, writing challenges, and writing opportunities that spurred their decision to take our courses. We explain that this initial reflection performs the forward and backward moves we will encourage throughout the semester (Taczak and Robertson). We want to learn about ways our students' preparation might enhance their experience in the courses and their hopes for the future. Equally importantly, we use this first writing assignment to introduce students to reflective discovery and the idea of linking past, present, and future learning.

Threaded-competency courses are inherently theory classes, and teachers may ask students to demonstrate understanding of theory through typical textual assignments. For example, because we teach theories of genre, our IPW students use these theories to write a genre analysis paper of a professional writing genre they choose—a fairly routine assignment in a writing class. However, a threaded-competency curriculum will purposely design each assignment with experiential learning in mind. As a result, even these more traditional assignments ask students to experiment with abstract knowledge by applying it to concrete situations and then to reflect on their learning. We next ask students to use and test what they learned from this assignment on the next assignment. So, for example, after writing the genre analysis paper, IPW students write a style guide document for the genre and then use a classmate's style guide to create a text in an unfamiliar genre.

This interplay between theoretical and experiential learning is the foundation of a threaded-competency course. While the experiential component will look different for every course, we share the following examples of experiential activities we have used to help teachers imagine activities appropriate to their own courses. In our IPW course, students experiment with and apply competencies by completing both traditional case studies and an open-case study in which they interact with an on-campus "client" (as described below). When they move to the APW course, practicing competency threads entails increased complexity and increased risk because students must complete a ten-hour per week professional writing internship. Still, students in both IPW and APW approach their learning in a back-and-forth process, moving recursively between class discussions, open-case studies, and internship experiences.

Following the Kolb cycle, we design readings and assignments that are relevant to students' concrete work experiences, which we use to illuminate and push students' understanding of the readings and in-class assignments. Every new experience requires students to evaluate how the situation is like and not like previous situations and to decide how theories and concepts apply or don't apply (Reiff and Bawarshi). This dialectic process helps students examine and refine their assumptions about the competencies. The semester-long APW internship gives students sustained engagement with professional writing tasks, allowing them to draw on earlier experiences in IPW and to transfer those experiences to more difficult client projects and more challenging team dynamics. Moving to higher-stakes tasks often forces students to critically question the theories they have learned and their assumptions about how communication works.

Below we describe extended examples of two elements of our threaded, competency-based approach to writing instruction. We selected two competencies we felt best exemplified the threaded approach, genre and leadership (see chart above). We offer this granular detail to illustrate the recursive nature of the threaded-competency curriculum and pedagogy. As we have taught our threaded-competency classes, we have discovered that this kind of curriculum can sometimes feel like messy pedagogy. It does not support neat, discrete instructional units that are completed in an orderly sequence. Nor does a threaded-competency approach provide clear signposts of when content has been "mastered"; instead, it signals the continual development and refinement of overlapping knowledge, skills, and dispositions. Rather than a model to follow, we hope the description below helps teachers in all WAC settings invent threaded-competency curricula that make sense for their courses.

Threading Genre Competency

Our courses introduce students to social action and rhetorical theories of genre that see genres as stabilized (for now) responses to recurring social situations. Students explore the idea that genres both respond to situations in ways that people deem successful and in turn shape those social situations. They learn to think of genre not just as formal features but as "the keys to understanding how to participate in the actions of a community" (Miller 85).

In IPW students apply those theories to contemporary professional writing situations and texts using a traditional case study format, but cases are culled from current events rather than textbooks. Students use the theory to identify and describe a recurring social situation, to evaluate the effectiveness of a genre's conventions in responding to the situation, to describe action the genre is trying to accomplish, and to imagine how the genre and the social situation might shift and shape each other. For example, during fall of 2018 when Tesla CEO Elon Musk was in the news for tweeting about taking his company public and smoking what appeared to be marijuana on television, students analyzed the company's press releases and blog posts using theories of the rhetorical situation (Bitzer, Vatz, Consigny) and genre (Miller, Devitt) to understand the company's response. During that same semester, students also analyzed statements from the Women's Tennis Association and United States Tennis Association that were posted on the organizations' Twitter accounts and websites in the wake of the dramatic US Open final between Naomi Osaka and Serena Williams. In fall 2019, students analyzed Boeing's professional writing in the aftermath of two 737 Max crashes, the grounding of all 737 Max planes, and Boeing CEO Dennis Muilenburg's testimony to Congress. Students analyzed how Boeing's professional writers used the genres of tweets, blogs, press releases, statements, and websites to shape fitting rhetorical responses to unfolding events. They evaluated those responses in terms of the action they accomplished and questioned whether the genre theories they learned adequately explained these examples of professional writing. They also created alternative responses, which in some cases imaginatively tested a genre's flexibility.

We believe that using current events as case studies allows students to experience theory (and appreciate its kairos) in a way that using textbook case studies does not. Our experience has shown that using current events makes students more eager to engage theory and more motivated to consider how theory helps them understand the world around them and their own lived experiences. Students sometimes feel compelled to correct or elaborate a theory that does not account for their interpretation of a situation. For example, students examining a letter to employees from Elon Musk that was posted on the company's website felt that the social action theories of genre we discussed in class didn't fully help them analyze a text that appeared to be written by Musk but that was likely written by someone else. The students' discomfort with the theory as an adequate explanation demonstrated that they were developing a disposition of curiosity as they sought more nuanced ways of understanding writers, writing situations, tasks, and texts.

IPW students also participate in open-case studies, using professional writing situations on campus as the material for their practice and concrete experiences. An open-case study model lets students apply their learning to a context—the university campus—where they already have "significant knowledge of their rhetorical situation and their probable readers" (Johnson-Sheehan and Flood 24). Because the campus is an "indeterminate, evolving rhetorical situation which [is] essentially unpredictable" (24), the open case studies allow students to apply theoretical knowledge to more richly complex situations than traditional case studies. Students' open-case study projects have included analyzing the directory for our campus's student union building. Based on their analyses, students produced a "deliverable" for the "client"—an interactive map app for the union building. Other open-case studies have resulted in a redesigned financial aid website, a grant proposal guide for a student-led non-profit agency affiliated with the business school, educational outreach materials for the dance department, marketing materials for a department minor, and a proposal for improving campus communication. As IPW students complete these open-case projects, they continue to apply, assess, and elaborate theory, while also practicing skills and dispositions.

The following semester in APW, students apply the same ideas about genre and rhetoric to create a "Needs Analysis" of their internship provider. The stakes for this assignment are higher than that of the IPW case studies because students meet with an actual supervisor and interpret the situational factors that influence what genres are most appropriate for addressing the company's content needs. Nevertheless, the students still use the rhetorical and genre theories (as well as skills and dispositions) they learned in IPW as they approach this new writing situation. After an initial meeting with the client, students draft an analysis of the rhetorical situation and genre and present that draft to the class for the others to critique. Each student presents their findings explaining both the organizational challenges they uncovered and their plan for addressing them. Teacher-led discussion helps the student reflect on their initial assumptions about the assessment, encouraging them to consider not only the stakeholder but the larger rhetorical situation and how that may impact their work at the company. The student and teacher feedback is designed to be constructive, but it can be directive at times, requiring the presenter to either defend a particular decision that may lack supporting evidence or to consider other possible workplace genres. These conversations between students and teacher require students to reflect on how well their knowledge of genre and rhetoric fits the new situation. In doing so, they often find that, as with the IPW case studies, their new experiences require them to reconceptualize abstract principles they have learned. The feedback process also allows students to demonstrate dispositions of creativity and flexibility as they adjust not just to the rhetorical situation but also to their peers' and teacher's responses to their plans for using genre to accomplish their purposes.

Threading Leadership Competency

Jonathan Alexander articulates leadership in the writing classroom as a "trans-literacy," that is a literacy practice more easily transferred because students see connections to the professional world (45, 46). Given the broad range of leadership models, we believe defining leadership for composition should include forms relevant to co-authored documents. We therefore define leadership using three criteria drawn from the literature: building a shared vision for the writing project, aligning resources to accomplish that vision, and acquiring commitment from the group to achieve that vision (Northhouse). We tell students that writing in professional contexts may require different leadership skills, and leadership may include being the project lead, or it may require leading through example throughout the life cycle of their projects.

Helping student-led writing groups set a vision for their project is an important first step. Our students often find themselves working in unfamiliar situations and with unfamiliar genres. This process begins by encouraging students to foster an environment where a diversity of ideas can be heard and where different group members can contribute. As students make time for vision setting, they develop stronger group dynamics which improve their collaborative efforts. Leadership in this context may require much less talking than what students initially think. In truth, we have seen those who are strong active listeners often help the group find a shared vision. Students are surprised by how much influence they have on a project if they can simply listen intently to what other group members say and then articulate areas of consensus and/or disagreement.

Mumford describes the second criteria of leadership as "idea structuring," a term which refers to an ability to offer specific feedback and help establish goals—which might include setting timeframes and expectations (737). We believe idea structuring is an essential skill for student-led collaborative writing projects because students often struggle with how to translate their ideas into project outcomes and how to productively challenge ideas that may not fit the agreed vision of the project. Teaching Mumford's notion of leadership gives students agency to help shape group discussion and a strategy for evaluating ideas as they relate to the goals of the project.

In both IPW and APW, students build a shared vision of their group writing project and practice idea structuring as they engage in different client projects. Again, "client" refers to both on-campus organizations (IPW) and off-campus organizations (APW). In preparation for these client projects, both courses introduce students to forms of leadership in collaborative writing and different approaches to project planning. After practicing using teamwork and project planning in addressing several case studies (including those mentioned above), IPW students turn to the on-campus client project, working in teams of three or four to complete a series of assignments that require them to link the conceptual knowledge they've gained through readings and case studies to the on-campus situation. Again, students use theories about rhetorical situations, genre, and discourse communities to understand the on-campus organization and its needs, the audience they will address, and the appropriate genre for their deliverable. But they also practice leadership as they collaboratively make every decision regarding choice of client, project design, process, and team roles. Students complete most assignments together: team contracts, research reports, proposals, final deliverables, and an oral presentation to a representative from the on-campus entity. Along the way, students individually compose progress memos and reflections on their learning, but the major work of the IPW client project is done collaboratively and invites students to practice idea structuring and setting a vision for the project.

The APW course allows students to continue to practice leadership competency in a complex, real-world situation. However, since the students have a formal relationship with an internship provider, the stakes are much higher. In the IPW class, students are essentially volunteering a service to the client, making them less accountable to the client than they are in an APW internship. In the APW course, students develop leadership competency in group-writing projects outside the classroom. For example, one APW student, assigned to a large data-software company, used Mumford's "establishing a shared vision" and "idea structuring" to propose and develop a new approach to proposal writing at the company. Sarah's internship placed her within a proposal writing team, and her particular role was to find better ways to train salespeople to be more self-sufficient proposal writers. While the proposal writing team mostly handled larger proposals, Sarah's internship focused on solving this particular workplace problem: help the sales team write their own proposals. Sarah reported feeling "overwhelmed the first few weeks," saying she didn't know much about business operations and complex software used by the different sales teams to coordinate their efforts. After some initial failures, she started to create a shared vision with her proposal writing team. In Sarah's words, she started to "feel like I was contributing to a definable solution."

After her initial needs analysis was complete, Sarah pitched an idea for a content library, a sort of copy-and-paste approach that sales people could use to create more informal proposals, proposals that would have the dual function of serving as scope documents for the client and company. The company was impressed with Sarah's vision for the project and integrated it into a larger content library where salespeople could go and copy and paste information requested in different requests for proposals, a common workplace document. Because of her success with her internship project, Sarah was offered a full-time position on the proposal writing team to help the company realize her vision for the project.

A Word about Reflection

Our courses thread both experiential and reflective learning activities across all competencies. We believe these pedagogical elements are essential for giving students opportunities to apply and test the competencies they develop in our courses. We see three primary benefits of active experimentation: (1) students strengthen their ability to think in abstract terms about their experiences and the skills those experiences demand; (2) students evaluate and refine the abstract ideas that are the foundation of each competency; (3) students intentionally practice competencies as a combination of knowledge, skill, and disposition. But we believe reflection is an equally essential component of our learning model because it helps students articulate connections between abstract concepts, the core professional competencies, and the particularities of the different contexts where they are practicing the competencies. We use reflective writing assignments, student conferences, and class discussions in both IPW and APW to ask students to reflect on their learning and experiences. We have found that student-led discussions in class, what we called "free discussions," are an especially productive means of reflection. These discussions allow students in both courses to explore problems with difficult clients or project management issues in a non-directive mode. The emphasis on non-directive student-led discussions allows us as teachers to move among the students, listening and observing the conceptualization process at work. Our students frequently express feelings of unbalance and disorientation associated with abstract conceptualization, but even these feelings can become rewarding learning opportunities when students engage in productive dialogue about how the theories they've learned help them make sense of problems in the coursework and the world beyond the classroom.

Because reflection in our classrooms is an iterative process and is always connected to both conceptual and experiential learning, it resembles Yancey's idea of "constructive reflection." It asks students to reflect cumulatively, not just about the many individual texts they write in both classes, but more importantly about the trajectory of their conceptual knowledge, their emerging skills, and their developing dispositions—in short, about the kind of writer they are becoming. As students draw on professional writing theories from class, they also begin to form their own ideas about professional writing and themselves as future professional writers.

We found that our experiential-reflective pedagogy accommodates a wide range of learners. The immersive, experiential portions of our courses seem to appeal to students who value concrete experience and active experimentation, while the in-class reflections and discussions appeal to students who are more comfortable with contemplation, observation, and abstract conceptualization. Additionally, the areas that students find less immediately comfortable or appealing provide opportunities for us as teachers to encourage and support their learning.

Concluding Thoughts: Transfer and the Threaded-Competency Curriculum

Our goal in the threaded-competency curriculum aims to help students use their theoretical knowledge, concrete experience, and reflective observations to become nimble and effective writers in any context. However, transfer is often difficult for students because it requires them to adapt recently acquired conceptual knowledge to new writing situations, which may challenge that knowledge. Spread over two semesters and encompassing a range of progressively more challenging situations, the threaded-competency curriculum provides students repeated opportunities to practice and reflect on their ability to transfer knowledge, skills, and dispositions. A threaded-competency curriculum means that we make competencies explicit and that we stay with them longer, giving students varied opportunities to practice and apply their learning to contexts with different levels of risk and reward. The low-stakes assignments of IPW, often ungraded and completed collaboratively in class, allow students to comfortably practice the competencies in preparation for the more unpredictable on-campus client project. In turn, the APW course's needs analysis assignment for a corporate client presents elevated risk and increased accountability, but it requires the same conceptual knowledge, skills, and dispositions learned in IPW.

Many times our students in the IPW and APW courses grasp theoretical ideas and see the value of the applied writing experiences, but they struggle to make the connection between the two. We've recognized that these struggles represent significant learning opportunities if students are given the time and opportunity for practice and reflection. The threaded-competency curricular approach embraces abstract conceptualization and active experimentation and provides repeated opportunities for students to practice, apply, and reflect on their learning experiences—including the disorientation that is an inevitable part of any experiential learning process. By requiring students to use competencies—knowledge, skills, and dispositions—to make sense of new experiences in and outside our classrooms, we help students build deeper connections to a broader system of knowledge about both professional writing and learning in general. Kolb describes this as transforming "observations into logically sound theories" (30). Our threaded-competency curriculum encourages a different style of learning than our previous courses did. In our new courses, curiosity is encouraged and frustration is expected as experiences fit (or don't fit) existing forms of knowledge. Rather than coming to a tidy conclusion, our threaded-competency courses help students see their learning as an ongoing process that extends beyond the end of a semester or the obtaining of a degree. By threading competencies and experiential learning through our courses, we wanted students to more consciously recognize the connections within each class, between our two-course sequence, and between their classroom experience and current and future experiences outside of the university. We believe that the design of our courses not only supports transfer but provides students with a model of how they might continuously engage in transferring competencies—knowledge, skills, and dispositions—to new contexts. Threading our professional writing courses with competencies and experiential-reflective learning activities gives students a framework for self-directed lifelong learning.

In that regard, the experience of creating these courses forced us as teachers and scholars to engage in the same process of transfer that we imagine for our students. We spent several months working collaboratively to formulate and articulate competencies as concepts, skills, and dispositions and to find a pedagogical approach that felt coherent for both of our courses and the workplace situations we envision our students entering. That process required us to draw on abstract concepts we had learned about teaching and learning, to apply them to the curricula we were developing, and often to reconceptualize our prior understanding to fit our new experiences and address our new goals. It also required us to strengthen (and in some cases develop) dispositions of flexibility, openness, and responsibility that our academic work does not always require. Thus, creating this threaded-competency curriculum engaged us in a learning process much like that we hope our students will experience as they take our courses. We can attest both to its moments of disorientation and frustration and to its potential to promote deep learning.

Works Cited

Alexander, Jonathan. "Gaming, Student Literacies, and the Composition Classroom: Some Possibilities for Transformation." *College Composition and Communication*, vol. 61, no. 1, 2009, pp. 35–63.

Barth, Benjamin S., and Ehren C. Bucholtz. "Threaded Introductory Chemistry for Prepharmacy: A Model for Pre-professional Curriculum Redesign." *Journal of Chemical Education*, vol. 94, no. 8, 2017, pp.106065.

Beaufort, Anne. *College Writing and Beyond: A New Framework for University Writing Instruction*. UP of Colorado, 2007.

Berkenkotter, Carol, and Thomas N. Huckin. "Rethinking Genre From a Sociocognitive Perspective." *Written Communication*, vol. 10, no. 4, 1993, pp. 475–509.

Bitzer, Lloyd F. "The Rhetorical Situation." *Philosophy and Rhetoric*, vol. 25, no. 1, 1968, pp. 1–14.

Consigny, Scott. "Rhetoric and Its Situations." *Philosophy and Rhetoric*, vol. 7, no. 3, 1974, pp. 175-86.

Council of Writing Program Administrators, et al. "Framework for Success in Postsecondary Writing." Jan. 2011, wpacouncil.org/files/framework-for-success-postsecondary-writing.pdf. Accessed 10 Nov 2018.

Cumbie-Jones, Claudia, "Threading a Sophomore Computer Animation Curriculum." *SIGGRAPH Computer Graphics*, vol. 35, no. 2, 2001, pp. 53–56. DOI=dx.doi.org/10.1145/563693.563708

Devitt, Amy J. "Genre Pedagogies." *A Guide to Composition Pedagogies*, 2nd ed., edited by Gary Tate, et al., Oxford UP, 2014, pp. 146–62.

—-. "Generalizing about Genre: New Conceptions of an Old Concept." *College Composition and Communication*, vol. 44, no. 4, 1993, pp. 573–86.

Duffy, John. *Provocations of Virtue: Rhetoric, Ethics, and the Teaching of Writing*. Utah State UP, 2019.

Engle, Randi A., et al. "How Does Expansive Framing Promote Transfer? Several Proposed Explanations and a Research Agenda for Investigating Them." *Educational Psychologist*, vol. 47, no. 3, 2012, pp. 215–31.

Fogarty, Robin. "Ten Ways to Integrate Curriculum." *Educational Leadership*, 1991, pp. 61–65.

Fogarty, Robin, and Judy Stoehr. *Integrating Curricula with Multiple Intelligences: Teams, Themes, and Threads*. IRI/Skylight Publishing, 1995.

Gee, James Paul. "A Sociocultural Perspective on Opportunity to Learn." *Assessment, Equity, and Opportunity to Learn*, edited by Pamela A. Moss et al., Cambridge UP, 2008, pp. 76–108.

Graff, Gerald. *Clueless in Academe: How Schooling Obscures the Life of the Mind*. Yale UP, 2003.

Guest, David. "The Hunt is on for the Renaissance Man of Computing." *The Independent* [London], 1991, p. 17.

Johnson-Sheehan, Richard, and Andrew Flood. "Genre, Rhetorical Interpretation, and the Open Case: Teaching the Analytical Report." *IEEE Transactions on Professional Communication*, vol. 42, no. 1, 1999, pp. 20–30.

Kolb, David A. *Experiential Learning: Experience as the Source of Learning and Development*, Prentice-Hall, 1984.

Kysilka, Marcella L. "Understanding Integrated Curriculum." *Curriculum Journal*, vol. 9, no. 2, 1998, pp.197–209.

Lewis, Deborah Y., et al. "QSEN: Curriculum Integration and Bridging the Gap to Practice." *Nursing Education Perspectives*, vol. 37, no. 2, 2016, pp. 97–100.

Markel, Mike. *Ethics in Technical Communication: A Critique and Synthesis*. Ablex Publishing, 2001.

Melzer, Dan. "The Connected Curriculum: Designing a Vertical Transfer Writing Curriculum." *The WAC Journal*, vol. 25, no. 1, 2014, pp. 78–91.

Meyer, Jan H. F., and Ray Land, editors. *Overcoming Barriers to Student Understanding: Threshold Concepts and Troublesome Knowledge*. Routledge, 2006.

Miller, Carolyn R. "Genre as Social Action." *Quarterly Journal of Speech*, vol. 70, 1984, pp. 151–67.

Moore, Jessie. "Mapping the Questions: The State of Writing-Related Transfer Research." *Composition Forum*, vol. 26, 2012.

Mumford, Michael D., et al. "Leading Creative People: Orchestrating Expertise and Relationships." *The Leadership Quarterly*, vol. 13, no. 6, 2002, pp. 705–50.

National Research Council. *How People Learn: Brain, Mind, Experience, and School: Expanded Edition*. National Academies Press, 2000.

Northhouse, Peter G. *Leadership: Theory and Practice*. 5th edition., Sage, 2010.

Nowacek, Rebecca S. *Agents of Integration: Understanding Transfer as a Rhetorical Act*. Southern Illinois UP 2011.

Perkins, David N., and Gavriel Salomon. "Are Cognitive Skills Context-Bound?" *Educational Researcher*, vol. 18, no. 1, 1989, pp. 16–25.

Reiff, Mary Jo, and Anis Bawarshi. "Tracing Discursive Resources: How Students Use Prior Genre Knowledge to Negotiate New Writing Contexts in First-Year Composition." *Written Communication*, vol. 28, no. 3, 2011, pp. 312–37.

Society for Technical Communication. "Ethical Principles" www.stc.org/about-stc/ethical-principles/. Accessed 10 Nov 2018.

Shaffer, David W. "Epistemic Frames for Epistemic Games." *Computers and Education*, vol. 46, no. 3, 2006, pp. 223–34.

Taczak, Kara, and Liane Robertson. "Reiterative Reflection in the Twenty-First-Century Writing Classroom: An Integrated Approach to Teaching for Transfer." *A Rhetoric of Reflection*, edited by Kathleen B. Yancey. Utah State UP, 2016, pp. 42–63.

Taylor, André, et al. "An Investigation of Champion-Driven Leadership Processes." *The Leadership Quarterly*, vol. 22, no. 2, 2011, pp. 412–33

Vatz, Richard D. "The Myth of the Rhetorical Situation." *Philosophy and Rhetoric*, vol. 6, no. 3, 1973, pp. 154–61.

Vetter, Matthew A., and Matthew J. Nunes. "Writing Theory for the Multimajor Professional Writing Course: A Case Study and Course Design." *Pedagogy: Critical Approaches to Teaching Literature, Language, Composition, and Culture*, vol. 18, no. 1, 2017, pp. 157–73.

von Oetinger, Bolka. "The Renaissance Strategist." *Journal of Business Strategy*, vol. 22, no. 6, 2001, pp. 38–42.

Wardle, Elizabeth. "Understanding 'Transfer' from FYC: Preliminary Results of a Longitudinal Study." *WPA Writing Program Administration*, vol. 31, no. 1–2, 2007, pp. 65–85.

Wiggins, Grant P., and Jay McTighe. *Understanding by Design*. Association for Supervision and Curriculum Development, 2005.

Yancey, Kathleen B. *Reflection in the Writing Classroom*. Utah State UP, 1998.
Yancey, Kathleen B., et al. *Writing Across Contexts: Transfer, Composition, and Sites of Writing*. Utah State UP, 2014

The Material Contexts of Writing Assignment Design

THOMAS POLK

> Scholarship on assignment design has largely concerned itself with the difficulty of designing effective writing assignments. While this research offers practical advice for instructors, it often overlooks important contextual factors that influence how writing assignments materialize. This research begins the work of contextualizing assignment design by reporting on interviews conducted with thirty-three faculty members who teach writing-intensive courses across the disciplines at George Mason University. Interviews prompted participants to describe the most pressing decisions they made while designing their assignments. Participants reported decisions related to the following five categories: promoting student agency, defining the writing task, scaffolding the process, clarifying communications, and navigating the institution. Findings from this study reveal that faculty decisions are frequently motivated by pedagogical intentions; however, this research also reveals that institutional and personal motivations exercise significant influence on decision-making.

This study investigates the situated decision-making of WID faculty as they design writing assignments, focusing particularly on the influences that faculty note most shape their designs. This research interest draws on two ongoing conversations in the field of writing studies. The first conversation centers on the professional writing that faculty practice as workers in institutional and disciplinary settings. John Swales (1996) opened this interest into what he called *occluded genres*, documents that faculty use "to support and validate the manufacture of knowledge" (p. 46). Swales believed that these documents were particularly important to study not only because of their commonality but also because these documents are regulated by local institutions with unpredictable expectations, making them complicated documents for outsiders and novices to compose. Since Swales's call, scholars have pursued this interest by focusing on genres that facilitate publication while others have increasingly called to expand this analysis to include such documents as syllabi, teaching statements, and retention-promotion-tenure reports (e.g., Baecker, 1998; Hyon, 2008; Fink, 2012; Neaderhiser, 2016).

The second conversation that informs this study focuses on a genre that is particularly important to the work of writing instruction: writing assignments. Writing studies' interest in assignments began in the 1970s with research by James Britton et al. (1975), who created a taxonomy to classify writing tasks in British secondary schools. This interest in description reached American contexts in the 1980s when Applebee, Auten, and Lahr (1981), Eblen (1983), and Bridgeman and Carlson (1984) studied various aspects of writing assignments in secondary and post-secondary contexts. More recent scholarship has turned toward advising faculty on best practices for design with particular attention paid to the characteristics of (in)effective assignments (Gardner, 2008; Harris, 2010; Anderson, Anson, Gonyea, & Paine, 2016). While this scholarship tells us a great deal about assignment design, their research perspectives often elide contextual nuance and demonstrate that we still have much to learn about assignment design.

In fact, Melzer (2014) observes, "few composition researchers have made [writing assignments] the focus of significant study" despite their ability to reveal "a great deal about their [instructors'] goals and values, as well as the goals and values of their disciplines" (p. 3). The latter part of Melzer's observation encourages scholars to recognize that writing assignments are not simply neutral documents that faculty use to elicit writing products but are the material distillations of our "pedagogical identities in action" (Neaderhiser, 2016, para. 28) capable of telling us much about the ways in which we teach writing because they materialize out of what Gardner (2008) calls the "full process," which includes everything from the invention of the assignment concept to the evaluation of the written product (p. 7–8). That is, writing assignments offer researchers a material site through which we can better understand how our pedagogical ideals become enacted in specific sites and situations of instruction.

In recognizing that assignments are not neutral documents, I also recognize that their sites of production are not neutral. That is, writing assignments are not just ideologically informed but also materially situated. I draw this perspective from Horner's (2000, 2016) framing of composition as a "material social practice" (2000, p. 59), which posits the practice of teaching writing as one inflected by the technologies, economic and physical conditions, and socio-institutional relations of those engaged in teaching and learning in specific sites. As such, the activity of teaching writing is formed not just by pedagogical aspirations but also the institutional conditions in which those aspirations are enacted. The problem, Horner argues, is that dominant representations of our work often overlook the institutionality of that work: "what we think we do, and what we think about what we do" often fail to capture the realities of our work because these representations are "separated from the material social conditions of its production, and so imagined as, at most, acting autonomously on, against, or in spite of but not with and within such conditions" (2016, p. 1; 2000, p. xvii).

Similarly, Scott (2009) argues that while writing studies scholars recognize the importance of context in understanding writing practices, "systematic connections" between materiality and pedagogy are "rarely made" in the field's literature (p. 7). He writes, "Though everyday institutional practices and the material terms of labor for teachers and students have a profound effect on the character of writing pedagogy, they don't often appear in research- or theory-driven discussions of postsecondary classroom pedagogy" (p. 7). Scott advocates for analyses that connect macro and micro perspectives of our work to better understand how everyday pedagogical practices dialectically engage institutional and broader discursive representations of those practices. From Scott's and Horner's theorizations, I draw a methodological impetus to investigate the complex and contradictory labor involved in what might otherwise be considered a mundane task: designing a writing assignment. Previous studies of assignment design typically elide this complexity because they focus on the *product* of design and not the *production* of design. My study intends, however, to begin describing assignment design as a "material social practice" and seeks to document how this central task of writing instruction is not only informed by pedagogical ideals but also inflected by institutional realities.

Thus, in the following article, I synthesize and extend conversations about assignment design by reporting on interviews conducted with thirty-three faculty members who teach writing-intensive courses across the disciplines at George Mason University (GMU). I begin with a brief review of the literature on writing assignments. This review reveals that research on assignment design largely fails to elicit insight from the people most involved in the design process: faculty members themselves. That is, few scholars have attended to the reason for studying occluded genres, as described by Swales: to better understand how local expectations shape and influence the production of these genres. While scholars who do research occluded genres typically focus on documentary materials, this study draws on interview data because of its ability to reveal the influences that most matter to participants. Taken together, studying writing assignments from the perspectives of faculty can tell us about not just about the values that instructors hold but also about the local realities of writing instruction and how those realities shape faculty (dis)engagement with the broader ideals of the field.

Following this review, I report on the methods of this study before discussing its major findings. The interviews used for this study focused on assignments that participants currently teach or have recently taught, and the questions sought to elicit participants' descriptions of the "full process." This report concentrates specifically on one question that prompted participants to describe the most pressing decisions they made while designing their assignments. Findings demonstrate that institutional and personal considerations have a significant influence on the design of assignments, and I conclude with a discussion of the importance of understanding context in assignment design.

Review: How Do Writing Studies Scholars Discuss Writing Assignment Design?

Research on writing assignments has typically discussed assignments in two ways: through descriptions of assignments and through prescriptions of effective design (best practices). Much of the early research on assignments was typically embedded in studies that sought to describe broader practices of writing instruction in university contexts. Studies by Eblen (1983) and Bridgeman and Carlson (1984) surveyed faculty about a variety of teaching practices, including how faculty defined the qualities of good writing, the importance of writing and particular writing skills for academics and professions, and the kinds of writing faculty typically assigned. These studies, and research on writing in high school contexts (Britton, 1975; Applebee, 1981), inform Melzer's more recent research on assignments across the disciplines (2003, 2009, 2014). Drawing on "2,101 writing assignments from 100 postsecondary institutions across the United States," Melzer provides a large-scale description of the purposes, audiences, and genres that faculty assign in academic writing contexts (2014, p. 6). Melzer reports that faculty design assignments with limited purposes and frequently prompt students to write to the teacher-as-examiner. In other words, faculty most frequently "ask students to display the 'right' answer or the 'correct' definition to the instructor through a recall of facts" (Melzer, 2003, p. 90), an assertion that echoes Eblen's research.

Perhaps because these descriptive studies demonstrate a lack of instructional practices generally promoted by writing specialists, Melzer (2014) and other scholars begin to think more seriously about what factors influence effective assignment design. Extending from his research design, for instance, Melzer suggests that WAC/WID specialists promote and "provide space" for particular types of writing; he specifically suggests more expressive and poetic writing that would better align with writing-to-learn pedagogies (2014, p. 116). However, most of Melzer's suggestions target WPAs about programmatic and curricular decisions, leaving the conversation of effective assignments to other scholars. Some of the more prominent research on effective design comes from Gardner (2008) and later Anderson, Anson, Gonyea, and Paine (2016) who draw on large national surveys to describe "effective" or "high impact" assignment design; most recently, Eodice, Geller, and Lerner (2016) shift the frame away from effective and toward "meaningful" writing assignments. The students who participated in their study suggest that meaningful writing occurs when they are able to make personal connections to the writing task, such as envisioning their future selves (2019). Collectively, while these scholars identify different characteristics, they largely advise that assignments should have clear expectations, prompt critical thinking, and enable student agency as core design elements.

Although this scholarship helps us to understand the potential tasks and content of ideal design, it doesn't help us understand how assignments (can) actually materialize in sites of instruction. And while it is useful to prescribe effective design practices, such scholarship overlooks how instructors navigate contextual influences that constrain their designs. It should be noted, however, that a few scholars have begun to investigate this relationship. For instance, Burlick (2011) considers the often-recommended design and pedagogical practice of providing choice to prompt, if not enable, student ownership over projects, a design recommendation repeated in the literature reviewed earlier. But, none of that scholarship considers how the context of K12 "high stakes" assessment constrains instructors' abilities to design assignments that might promote student agency. As scholars, we should consider the implications of those competing interests: how much space does an instructor have to promote these design practices when students are compelled to take tests that offer little control over topic, process, and/or product? Research by Thaiss and Zawacki (2006) performs a more thorough theorization of the relationship between context and assignment design in their study of disciplinary writing practices. Based on their findings, Thaiss and Zawacki theorize that a mixture of contexts influences faculty perceptions of academic writing and teaching, and they identify these as the academic, the disciplinary, the subdisiplinary, the institutional, and the idiosyncratic. Thaiss and Zawacki offer these five contexts as a heuristic for clarifying the values and expectations implied in the language used to design assignments and evaluate written products, but their research also opens up the possibility for researchers to think more seriously about the role of context in teaching.

In sum, this brief review suggests that research on assignment design has largely not attended to faculty members' own perspectives on the ways in which contexts shape our field's knowledge into their local practices, if those practices are shaped by writing studies in the first place. With the exception of work by Burlick (2011), Thaiss and Zawacki (2006), and Eodice, Geller, and Lerner (2016 & 2019), research on assignment design has adopted an etic perspective, failing to elicit insight from the people most involved in the design process: writing instructors. While the field of writing studies has a good sense of what it considers ideal design, it doesn't yet have rich descriptions of the ways in which contextual forces effect that ideal. For this reason, the remainder of this paper reports on interviews conducted with thirty-three faculty members who teach writing intensive courses at GMU.

Methods: Talking with Faculty About Their Assignments

While both Burlick (2011), and Thaiss and Zawacki (2006) help us to begin the necessary work of thinking about assignment design in context, the above review suggests that there are yet more questions and contexts to explore. Consider, for instance, Thaiss and Zawacki's (2006) observation that faculty often conceive of student writing through specific disciplinary conventions but often fail to articulate the underlying disciplinary knowledge when talking about writing assignments with students; this finding is also asserted by Clark (2005). The gap of disciplinary and writing knowledge between students and faculty can often result in the failure of assignment design and the production of student writing that can be harshly evaluated by faculty. Thaiss and Zawacki write, "When very real differences are cloaked in the language of similarity, it's understandable that students would find it hard to decode what teachers want" (p. 59). In light of this observation, how should and do faculty consider a design suggestion to create assignments with "clear writing expectations" (Anderson, Anson, Gonyea, & Paine, 2016, p. 5)? Thaiss and Zawacki would suggest that their heuristic would help faculty clarify their language and expectations, but that advice assumes that faculty are actually concerned with developing clear writing instructions. Thus far, research on assignment design hasn't documented this interest or why in fact faculty would feel compelled to clarify their instructions if they do. Given this lack of documentation, the current study seeks to explore the following questions:

> Q1: What decisions do faculty describe as their most pressing when designing assignments?
>
> Q2: What influences do faculty report shape these decisions?

The interviews used to address these questions were collected as part of a larger research project at GMU locally known as the Re/View Project. This ongoing review of upper-level writing instruction attempts to better understand the everyday activities and needs of the university's students, faculty, and administrators. In collaboration with GMU's WAC program, a team of graduate research assistants has collected survey data, conducted sixty interviews, observed a number of classrooms, and amassed a significant corpus of instructional documents, including assignment sheets and syllabi.

The current study focuses on a particular set of interviews conducted during the spring of 2018 that concentrated on assignments participants either were currently teaching or had recently taught. Interview participants represent eight of the nine colleges that offer undergraduate courses at GMU and range in employment appointments from graduate teaching assistantships to fully tenured professorships. These faculty were recruited through emails sent to all faculty who teach writing-intensive courses and through professional development workshops for faculty who teach upper-level research and writing courses. The interview questions sought a range of information about the pedagogical and writing backgrounds of participants, but the majority of questions focused on one specific assignment or sequence of assignments, which interviewers collected before the interviews and used as a focal point for questions and responses during them. The interviews were designed to document the relationship between the material assignments and the contextual influences that shaped what appeared on the page and that were of particular significance to participants.

To identify data that responds to my specific research questions, I began coding the interviews descriptively, pulling language that participants used to describe the *specific decisions that they made* and *the reasoning that informed those decisions*. Upon reviewing my initial codes, I observed that many of the *specific decisions* participants discussed resonated with the language used in the scholarship on effective assignment design reviewed earlier. As my review of this literature revealed, these studies promote similar considerations and employ similar language to talk about effective design. In fact, three of my codes come almost directly from Gardner's suggested process for developing writing assignments: "define the writing task, explore the expectations, [and] provide the supporting materials and activities" (2008, p. 36). I kept *defining the task*, revised *explore the expectations* to *clarifying communications*, and revised *supporting materials and activities* to *scaffolding the process*. Eodice, Geller, and Lerner's (2016) research on meaningful writing inspired my fourth code, *promoting agency*, and my fifth code, *navigating the institution*, derived from Burlick's (2011) and Thaiss and Zawacki's (2006) research on context. I, thus, grouped my codes into the following categories:

- **Defining the Task:** pertaining to defining the purpose of the assignment, the type of writing to be produced, requirements of the student text, and the evaluation of the text.
- **Clarifying Communication:** pertaining to effective communication of the assignment, its process, and faculty expectations.
- **Scaffolding the Process:** pertaining to the timing of the assignment and the kinds of supporting activities and materials.
- **Promoting Agency:** pertaining to making the assignment relevant, relatable, and meaningful to the student. Also includes considerations of challenge and student efficacy.
- **Navigating the Institution:** pertaining to decisions about institutional and departmental requirements and matters.

To categorize *the reasoning that informed the decisions*, I largely drew from Thaiss and Zawacki's (2006) heuristic of the five contexts through which faculty talk about academic writing; these contexts are the academic, the disciplinary, the subdisciplinary, the institutional, and the idiosyncratic or personal. I originally used these same five categories to organize my codes but felt a tension about how well these categories described and explained what I was observing. They did not seem to accommodate the experiences with teaching and students that faculty often referred to, and I recognized this tension as pivoting on the difference in research intentions: Thaiss and Zawacki focused on how the writing practices of faculty members informed their assignments; my current interest is less tightly focused. While the academic writing practices of faculty certainly inform their pedagogies, so too do other factors, such as their experiences teaching and interacting with students. So, I revised Thaiss and Zawacki's five contexts slightly: I kept the *disciplinary* and *institutional* categories in place, but I merged the *subdisciplinary* category into the *disciplinary*; I refocused the *idiosyncratic* onto the *personal* to reflect the fact that these interviews reveal the decision-making related not only to faculty values and beliefs but also to embodied individuals; and I redefined the *academic* as *pedagogical* to capture my participants' experiences not with writing in the academy but with teaching (writing) in the academy. This last category also draws definition from the prescriptive and descriptive studies on assignment design. Thus, my final four categories are described below:

- **Disciplinary:** "pertaining to the methods and conventions of the teacher's broad field" and specific concentration(s) (Thaiss & Zawacki, 2006, p. 138).
- **Institutional:** "pertaining to the policies and practices of the local school and department" (Thaiss & Zawacki, 2006, p. 138).
- **Pedagogical:** pertaining to the perceptions of pedagogy and prior experiences with teaching, learning, and students.
- **Personal:** pertaining to the individual's values, beliefs, and embodiment.

A potential limitation of the interview protocol hinges on how participants understand what constitutes a *writing assignment*. Some faculty might perceive *assignment* to simply refer to the document given to students, but I believe this concern is mitigated by the extensive set of questions designed to elicit the processes that enact and pedagogies that underlie the documents. Despite this potential limitation, I believe that my study offers useful findings that can further discussions of assignment design particularly because they draw from interviews, a method seldom used in this research. That is, the current study deepens the ongoing conversation about assignment design because the interviews add granularity seldom reported.

Findings: Faculty Talk About the Most Pressing Decisions They Made While Designing Their Assignments

On first glimpse, many of the decisions faculty made while designing their assignments might seem to be only concerned with the texts that they are creating (the assignment sheet) and/or the texts that they are eliciting from their students, so many of my participants responded that their decisions were about textual requirements. These decisions were often framed either tacitly or explicitly as a "constant balancing act," which is how Participant 7 described his thinking about page requirements. Inspired by Participant 7's observation, the following descriptions reveal how participants in this study negotiated the various contextual influences that shape the materialization of their writing assignments. This section is divided into two parts: first, I describe findings related to the *specific decisions* participants made; second, I describe the participants' *reasons for making those decisions*. This second section will include some representative quotations from participants to demonstrate the nuances elided by categorizing their responses.

Q1: What decisions did faculty describe as their most pressing?

Figure 1 displays the categories of decisions that faculty members made while designing their assignments. The chart identifies the total number of decisions, not participants; that is, some participants discussed multiple decisions. The largest category, which more than doubled the next most common, was *defining the task*. Within this category, seven participants cited decisions about text length as their most pressing, six were concerned with questions of evaluation, three cited decisions about how the project would align with course goals, two cited decisions about the kind of text to assign, and two others listed deliberations about citations as most pressing.

The second most frequently discussed decisions related to the process structuring the assignment and the communication about the assignment. Participants cited eleven decisions related to *scaffolding the process* as their most pressing. The decisions in this category varied widely and included deliberations about peer reviews, invention activities, the sequence of assignments, and the amount of time available for assignments. Participants also discussed their attempts at *clarifying communications* about their assignments eleven times. They largely were concerned with their students' ability to understand what the assignment prompted them to do.

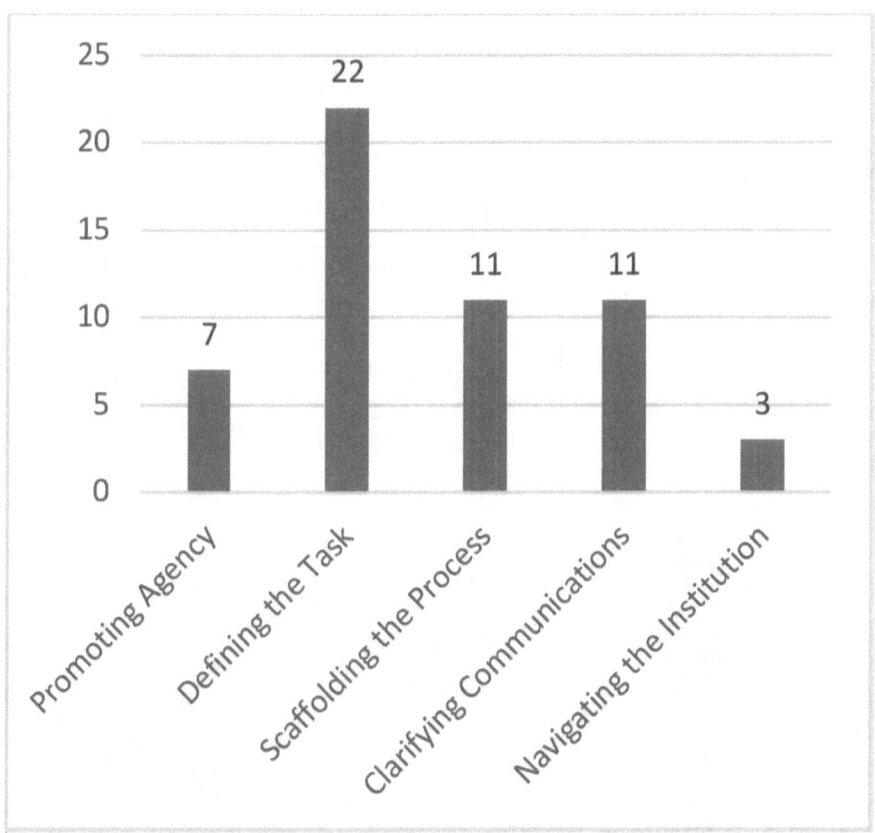

Figure 1. Categories of decisions identified by faculty as most pressing

The least commonly cited decisions related to student agency and the institution. Participants named *promoting agency* as a core decision in their deliberations seven times, and they seemed to approach the design process in the way that many of writing studies scholars would hope: thinking about how to make the assignment meaningful, relatable, relevant, and possible for their students. This category, however, resurfaces in discussions about the influences that shape other decisions listed here. Finally, three participants identified issues with *navigating the institution* as most pressing. Of these three participants, one discussed decisions about staffing, the second discussed decisions about enrollment, and the third discussed decisions related to the curriculum. Two of these participants, however, should not be seen as typical instructors as their interview responses reveal privileged status within the institution. Participant 18, who cited staffing as her central concern, also coordinates the course for her department and is responsible for staffing its sections, and

Participant 10 admits that his department permits him control over the enrollment of his course; that is, he is allowed to set the enrollment below what most WI courses can. Participant 13, however, is a new instructor (also adjunct) who confessed that she simply needed to understand the purpose of the course and the syllabus that she was given to teach.

Q2: What influences did faculty report shaped these decisions?

Figure 2 details the four main categories of influences that participants reported. It should be noted that these numbers correspond with the number of reasons given, not the number of faculty giving those reasons; that is, faculty often offered multiple reasons for their decisions. The discussion below includes some representative quotations, which are lightly edited to enhance readability.

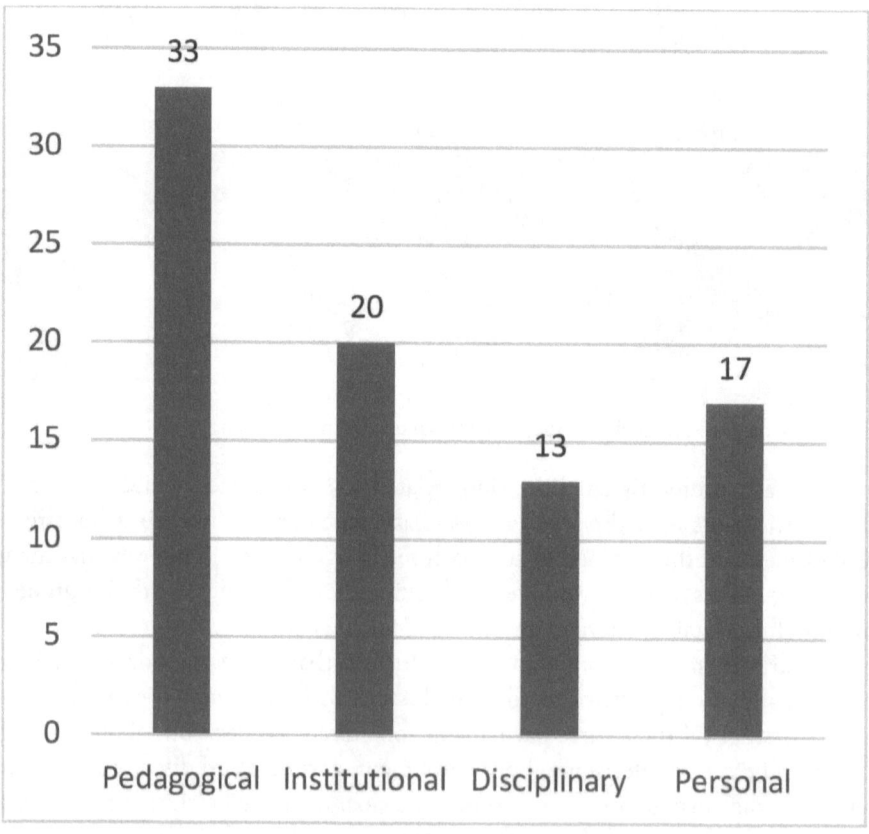

Figure 2. Categories of contexts identified by faculty as influencing their decisions

The most frequently cited reason pertained to *pedagogical* concerns; in all, participants cited thirty-three reasons for the decisions that they made. The decisions in this category were influenced most frequently by concerns for student agency; in fact, thirteen faculty members were concerned with making the assignment meaningful, giving students choice, and/or helping students feel capable of successfully completing the assignment, as Participant 34 demonstrates: "are they going to be capable of doing it?" He continues, "You want to challenge them, but you can't overburden them; you want to get them to do good research and good quality thinking, but yet you don't expect them to write publishable work." Later, he adds, "Do I want this pristine perfect paper that I read that brings tears to my eyes cause it's so beautiful, or do I want to give them an opportunity to take a stab at something difficult and not get there but learn on the way?" Finally, Participant 34 reveals that this question derives from what he sees as a central question plaguing education today: grade inflation and the pressures to earn or award high marks: "That seems like one of the problems in education today is that everybody has to get an A. I know that grade inflation is almost a cliché thing now, but it's true the pressure from everybody especially from the students; and the pressure they put on themselves is that they have to get an A or somehow they've failed."

Another particularly interesting thread in the *pedagogical* category, and one that seems related to participant 34's concerns, were questions about challenge and the independence of students; three faculty members described this as a decision between supporting or guiding students and fostering their reliance upon that support which would, in effect, impede their growth. Participant 21 represents this reasoning when she discusses her decision to include checklists with peer review activities. She explains:

> There is part of me that wonders: am I facilitating their learning so that when they need to go and do some kind of writing or thinking assignment like this in the future they're able to do it without these things in place, or am I creating something that's sort of like a crutch? Then they're not going to be able to do these things in the future without somebody saying, "you gotta do this and then this and then this?" And that is something that I struggle with internally: are we enabling students to become better writers? Are we enabling them to need all these things where somebody's saying this is what you need to do? And I don't know the answer.

It should be noted that her deliberations are also mediated by her conception that students aren't very good at reviewing their own work and aligning that work with assignment instructions and materials. This trend of basing decisions on prior experiences with students and teaching was also common in this category. Sadly, many of these discussions interpreted students in rather negative ways or contrasted them through discussions of student "range," a common theme that prior research at GMU revealed faculty perceived as a major constraint to their teaching (LaFrance & Polk, 2018).

The second most frequently cited category of reason concerned *institutional policies and practices*. Of the twenty references to this category, participants most frequently identified their own lack of agency in decision-making; in total, ten participants confessed that the decisions they grappled with were actually already decided upon by departmental policies. A majority of these faculty taught with prescribed assignments and curricula. An additional two participants cited WAC program criteria as the driver behind their decisions. Participants, however, demonstrated interesting means for justifying or operationalizing agency within these parameters. For instance, Participant 14 reveals that her college requires rubrics for assignments, but she recognizes the affordances of such a practice: "I was forced to do a rubric, but I think it's useful. I have to say it helps to explicate my expectations and how I'm going to grade." She explains how she uses the rubric to help students understand the citation practices in her discipline:

> But what I also do in the rubric is I say to them: use three sources here, find a couple sources here, find a source here. So that now I'm directing them that they actually have to source not just the topic or the policy, but they have to source their theory and they have to provide a citation for their methods. . . . They understand that when they're building their writing. Their review of the literature is much more complex.

Similarly, Participant 32 discusses her negotiation of a required rubric, first believing it to be "nonsense" but later recognizing that the rubric also protects her agency as an evaluator and frees her to grade artifacts as she deems appropriate: "It really protects the professor." She believes that the assignment rubric removes the "question of subjectivity on my part" and eases the process of responding to students' questions about grades. Participant 32's comment resonates with Participant 34's earlier remarks about grade inflation and gives reason to appreciate the complexity of a departmental policy and its anonymous power, which is sometimes liberating (as expressed here) and sometimes constraining (as described below).

Participant 13, mentioned earlier, shows another dimension to the complexity of departmental practices when she reveals that she spent a significant amount of energy simply trying to understand the course, its syllabus, the "big picture, and then be able to relay it to the students." She felt that this was important because she needed to "sell the course" to the students:

You've got students who are waiting to be negative, so you don't want to appear negative; you want them to see the big picture. It all comes together, and I keep trying to share that information with them. Last semester was a little more difficult because some of the things I was like, "Why are we doing this? It's not really necessary." This is what I was personally saying. So, the message I was sharing with them was probably not the message I was sharing with myself.

One other faculty member, Participant 7, reveals how institutional policies can further influence decisions about teaching. When discussing his decision about page requirements and the amount of writing he would require from his students, Participant 7 reveals his motivation: "I think it was one of my salary reviewers actually . . . they thought I didn't ask for enough writing for my students; [it] was like a critique of my teaching. . . . So, I think one semester I upped the writing for this [assignment] because of that." While we might consider the addition of writing in a writing-intensive course as a positive, this participant had just been reflecting on the balance between student agency and the amount of work he required, something he referred to as a "constant balancing act." As he finishes his thought that began with the reference to the salary reviewers, he begins to interpret that balancing act as a matter of student labor versus quality: "I can ask them to write an extra page or two just for the hell of it, and reading the student essays: am I actually getting value from those extra two pages or not, right? . . . Those were the two things I was thinking about word length."

The least frequently cited category pertained to *disciplinary* concerns. In all, eleven participants cited thirteen deliberations that were framed through their disciplines. These concerns included questions about paper topics, disciplinary genres, and the professional habits of writers and workers in the respective fields. Of these, the habits of professionals were most frequently cited, as demonstrated by Participant 4. He cited his most pressing decision as page length but quickly began a conversation about the sequencing of assignments in the semester. Ultimately, he reveals that he changed the type of writing in an early assignment (used as scaffolding for the major writing assignment that anchored the interview) in order to have his students "start thinking like a project manager as soon as I can."

Participant 11 joins this consideration with another theme in this category: familiarity with the writing practices of the profession. His decision to promote student agency by offering choice over product reveals that Participant 11 wants his students to decide on that product based upon the area of writing that they are least comfortable with:

Because some students need to learn more in general about what the form of a screenplay looks like, and others need to learn more in general; they might be perfect writers from a form standpoint, but they're not imaginative at all with content, or not as imaginative with content. So, there's that general divide between strengths. But then also, on a script-by-script basis, the needs would dictate one or the other. So, the student who's adapting a novel for the first time, she needs to do research into the adaptation process because that's the biggest deficit.

Participant 16 uses this theme to emphasize the importance of correctness to his students. He states that errors in grammar, spelling, and mechanics undermine the function of a genre in his discipline because that genre typically is the first connection many professionals make with one another. That is, his decision about grade weights relies on his belief that "everything needs to be perfect because sometimes your first impression of somebody is going to be a piece of paper." He continues to explain, writing a proposal "is essentially a job interview. They ask you, submit a proposal. Your proposal IS YOUR INTERVIEW for the job."

The final category, and the third most frequently cited, pertains to decisions motivated by *personal* concerns for either the instructors or students impacted by the decisions being made. In all, ten participants cited seventeen reasons for decisions they made while designing their assignments. The codes in this category, however, largely refer to considerations of student and faculty labor and the emotions tied to that labor. Overall, five of the ten participants included in this category express seven reasons for decisions that are tied to faculty labor (both in and outside of the course), another five cite six reasons tied to student labor (both in and outside of the course), and two participants cite three reasons related to faculty emotion that informed their decision-making. Participant 12 articulates the most direct connection between concerns for labor and decisions about assignment design when he talks about his deliberations over page length: "Length of the paper is another big one. What are my expectations in terms of length? I settled on 5 to 7 pages because of how many students that I have. And the grading load that I have with that." Participant 10 adds to this observation and multiplies his concern for labor over several courses:

> Between the two classes, [I] have an enrollment that's up there collectively; that sort of pressures me to do more or less in terms of the time I can spend reviewing and editing and commenting on what they've done. Just because of the time that's required. Obviously, the fewer the students the more time I can spend on that.

It should be noted here that Participant 10's decision was about lowering enrollment caps, something that his department permits but is unique for WI instructors at my institution. Therefore, his testimony could be argued to carry extra weight for issues of labor in other courses taught by instructors who don't have the ability to limit their enrollments.

While concern for labor was the most frequently cited in this category, two participants did mention concerns for their emotions. Participant 19 admits that she selects paper topics based on her own personal interests, and Participant 3 sequences his assignments to avoid "mind-numbing" bouts with grading. In fact, Participant 3 demonstrates how quickly concerns for emotion can slide into concerns over labor. When talking about considerations of scheduling, he explains, "I'm also trying to mix these assignments up a little bit; I also try to think in advance about how far behind I'm going to fall in the grading, and how guilty I'm going to feel about falling that far behind in the grading."

The other most frequently mentioned reason in this category derived from concerns for student labor: both the workload that faculty felt students were capable of handling and their observations of student responsibilities outside of the classroom and university. Participant 19 confides that she directly considers the amount of work students are completing in the class when she decides on page length requirements: "So I wanted to make sure that this assignment was appropriate in length given the amount of work that they're also doing in the course." Participant 7 demonstrates how this concern impacts the sequencing of assignments throughout the semester:

> I think the decisions have gone into how much time I'm expecting students to devote to doing this, right? And then that's played into . . . what kind of preparatory steps I do in class or not. [...] I think that's the thing that weighs kind of heaviest on my mind as I'm thinking about juggling assignments . . . is how much labor [and] time I'm expecting from students.

Finally, participants expressed concerns over the responsibilities students have outside of the classroom. Participant 28 reveals that his design decisions are impacted by his students' obligations to earn money, which impacts not only how he tries to align his assignment with the course goals but also his expectations for what they (can) produce:

> We've done a tremendous disservice by increasing the tuition rates for our students so much that they are trying to work huge numbers of hours, and they just don't have the expectation or the required time to do as well as they could in background and in research. And in that case, my expectation levels of them in the past have been more along the lines of what I expect from

graduate students in terms of time commitment and efforts, and I think that that's eroded over time; it's very difficult to have those levels of expectations because very good students come in tears and say I have to work 60 hours a week at Foot Locker to survive.

Conclusion: Recognizing the Complexity of Assignment Design

This study documented the assignment design practices of thirty-three writing instructors at George Mason University, and it sought to record the most pressing decisions these faculty members made while designing their assignments and the reasons that animated their ultimate design decisions. This research focus developed out of the recognition that much of the literature on assignment design overlooked the perspectives of those who are best able to tell us about the actual practice of design: writing instructors themselves. While much of our scholarship on assignment design describes what faculty produce and provides useful accounts of best practices, hearing directly from faculty about what influences their designs helps writing specialists better understand the local nuances subtending this pedagogical practice and the contextual influences that complicate, if not impede, ideal design. These findings should serve as a reminder that the specific decisions faculty make are often part of a larger, more complex framework of deliberation that extends beyond a singular focus on the pedagogical. Before addressing this point at more length, however, I would like to consider a few practical implications this research suggests for WAC specialists.

First, the findings reinforce the importance of talking with faculty across the disciplines about the differences (and overlaps) between writing-to-learn and learning-to-write, a conversation so fundamental to WAC that Anson (2015) identifies it as a threshold concept. A number of the faculty in this study reported struggling with decisions of evaluation: were they supposed to grade student writing based upon the replication of an idealized written product or were they supposed to encourage students to explore content more freely? These decisions don't have to be mutually exclusive, but the deliberation points to an opportunity for WAC specialists to talk with faculty about different approaches to using writing, the goals that those approaches can serve, and the implications for evaluation. When WAC specialists help faculty to understand these two fundamental approaches, it can ease other decisions faculty make, such as their strategies for providing feedback and concerns over content coverage.

Second, a finding of this study is that faculty are frequently concerned with the clarity of their designs, but this finding raises questions about the concept of *clarity* and what it means in the context of assignment design. In this study, one-third of the participants confided that they deliberated the most about clarifying their assignments with the hope that a clear assignment might improve student performance. These deliberations align with Anderson et al.'s (2016) research on effective design when they advise faculty to "provide students with an accurate understanding" (p. 5) of the writing task. This alignment, however, prompts the question: what provides that accurate understanding? The participants in this study seemed to believe, at least partly, that the assignment sheet itself provided students with clarity. But should we think of clarity only in terms of the document, or does clarity concern something larger than the document? And how does the expectation of learning, with the implications of novelty and challenge, complicate conceptions of clarity in assignment design? In my own teaching experience, I find students can often be confused when I first assign a project; they aren't always certain of the process or the product. That confusion fades as we work on the project and negotiate our collective understanding of it. Does that mean my prompts are not well-written? Is the scaffolding and instruction that effective? When and where does confusion turn to comfort or clarity for both faculty and students?

Both Gardner (2008) and Anderson et al. (2016) advise instructors to make writing assignments interactive: to talk with students about expectations, to listen to their interpretations, and to negotiate the distances. Those suggestions imply clarity might be the result of an instructional process more so than the quality of a document. How can WAC specialists help writing instructors expand their conceptions of clarity accordingly? And how can we help them gauge what a productive level of uncertainty might look like? In faculty development programming, WAC specialists might use modeling for this purpose. For example, WAC specialists could demonstrate for faculty how to negotiate understandings of an assignment by sharing student planning documents and reflections on assignments or summarizing the kinds of discussions we have with students as assignments progress. This kind of modeling might persuade faculty of the importance of teaching writing as a process, provide them with some specific language for facilitating classroom conversations about writing, and emphasize the value of reflection for learning. In this way, the interest in clarity offers WAC specialists an opportunity to talk with faculty about concerns larger than the assignment sheet and to move them away from seeing clarity as a matter of document design towards seeing clarity as a matter of instructional design. The larger takeaway here should be, however, that the specific deliberations identified in this research and present in our programs, such as clarity, provide entry points into meaningful faculty development that brings research on best practices into conversation with the everyday realities that faculty navigate.

Third, the findings provide a glimpse into how some faculty perceive standardized instructional materials, but this glimpse begs for more attention. Ten participants reported that their most pressing decisions were already made for them by departmental or institutional policies requiring them to adopt certain practices or use specific materials. Unsurprisingly, some of these faculty resisted the requirements, at least initially. Both Participant 32 and 14 confided their displeasure when they first learned about the requirements, but they eventually recognized the affordances offered by the materials. Participant 14, in particular, remarked how using a college-required rubric improved her communications with her students about the assignment; similarly, Participant 32 felt the departmental rubric she used improved her grading process. However, Participant 13 talked at length about her struggles with the materials she was given to teach; she felt they were out of touch with professional practice and spent an incredible amount of energy simply trying to understand how they helped prepare students for work in her profession. This finding reinforces the importance of communicating the goals of required materials with faculty and hints at the potential impact that this kind of communication might have on classroom instruction. It should also remind WAC specialists and administrators to systematically listen to and learn from the daily experiences of faculty as they teach with standardized materials.

These participants' experiences should also prompt us to think more expansively about agency. Scholarship on assignment design frequently promotes the importance of student agency and its relationship to student performance. Eodice, Geller, and Lerner (2016), for instance, discuss agency as one of the cornerstones of the meaningful writing experiences they document. What might a focus on faculty agency reveal about the ways in which faculty prompt writing and students experience it? That is, how does faculty agency impact student performance? Here, I am particularly reminded of Participant 7's deliberation over page lengths and student labor. While he believed the amount of writing he originally intended to assign would not overwhelm his students and would enable them to produce quality writing, Participant 7 extended the length of the assignment to satisfy his "salary reviewer's" comment to add more writing to the course. His experience and the experiences of Participants 14 and 32 (detailed above) suggest a complex relationship between faculty agency and student experiences: the limitations on Participant 7's agency seem to negatively impact the writing that students will experience in his course while the constraints placed on Participants 14 and 32 seem to enhance the classroom instruction. Thus, future research might consider how instructors and administrators balance professional expertise with curricular vision and institutional policies. Research by Gere et al. (2015) offers a compelling look at the relationship between a program's requirements and its stakeholders, and scholars might add to their study by considering how program and institutional policies support, limit, or create agency and how faculty and administrators negotiate that agency within institutional constraints.

Finally, the participants in this study revealed how complicated designing (and teaching) an assignment can be. Participants identified a number of expected reasons for their decision-making, such as the desire to promote disciplinary habits; they also revealed some surprising reasons, such as the need to satisfy the desires of a salary reviewer. Importantly, the participants in this study showed that they often make decisions about teaching based on non-pedagogical and non-disciplinary concerns. In other words, they reveal that assignment design is an activity in which pedagogical intentions are often in conflict with the material conditions of their enactment. Participant 9 perhaps best demonstrates the complex and contradictory work observed in this study. Her deliberations over page length represent how the four contexts identified here impact seemingly basic design decision-making, turning it into what she and others identify as a "constant balancing act" (Participant 7). During her interview, Participant 9 reveals that she is reconsidering the number of pages that she expects for a background section in an assigned research report. She states that the disciplinary conventions would suggest a two to three-page limit, but her experience with students also influences her thinking: "students aren't good at writing concisely yet . . . if you limit it to two to three, would they get everything in that they need? But then the flipside of that is, by making it three to four, am I encouraging them to puff it up by not practicing concise writing?"

This deliberation turns toward a more general question of pedagogy discussed earlier: how to provide enough guidance without being too prescriptive and encouraging student dependence on external support. Participant 9 wants to give her students enough freedom to fail so that she can "get to that teachable moment" when she helps students learn from their own mistakes, a sort of trial-and-error, experience-based pedagogy frequently referenced by participants. During this deliberation, she also considers how the length requirement of this section impacts how the overall project satisfies the institutional expectations as they are expressed through the program requirements (here, word count); she jokes about the authority of institutional influence, "Not that I think anybody is going to like arrest me if I don't, but we do want to be responsible for meeting what we said we would do." She ultimately decides on four pages. When asked why she makes this decision, she responds: "Oh well, that's probably self-preservation more than anything else."

Deliberating over page length requirements might seem mundane, but it reveals real impacts on the kinds of instruction faculty (feel able to) deliver. These impacts include manipulating the conventions of disciplinary and professional genres and sacrificing pedagogies and practices that faculty believe to be effective (e.g., a design imperative to prompt agency might be complicated by concerns for labor). This finding reveals the power that local contexts exercise over disciplinary notions of pedagogy. Of the eighty-three reasons motivating the design decisions described in this article, thirty-three were based on pedagogy; only thirteen were rooted in disciplinary contexts. The remaining thirty-seven originated in either institutional or personal contexts, accounting for forty-five percent of the reasons offered. That prompts a real need to understand assignment design as a "material social practice" (Horner, 2000, p. 59), one that might be informed by national conversations of pedagogy but one that is definitely shaped by local conditions. This finding also suggests that some of the most impactful faculty development work WAC specialists can do is at the institutional level: listening to and learning from the lived experiences of faculty; recognizing and rewarding faculty for the labor involved in good writing instruction; and advocating, securing, and maintaining fair labor conditions for faculty (and students).

References

Anderson, P., Anson, C. M., Gonyea, R., & Paine, C. (2016). How to create high-impact writing assignments that enhance learning and development and reinvigorate WAC/WID programs: What almost 72,000 undergraduates taught us. *Across the Disciplines, 13*(4), 18 pp. https://wac.colostate.edu/docs/atd/hip/andersonetal2016.pdf.

Anson, C. M. (2015). "Crossing thresholds: What's to know about writing across the curriculum." In L. Adler-Kassner & E. Wardle (Eds.), *Naming what we know: Threshold concepts of writing studies* (pp. 203-219). Utah State University Press.

Applebee, A. N., Auten, A., & Lehr, F. (1981). *Writing in the secondary school: English and the content areas*. NCTE.

Baecker, D. L. (1998). Uncovering the rhetoric of the syllabus: The case of the missing I. *College Teaching, 46*(2), 58–62.

Bridgeman, B., & Carlson, S. B. (1984). Survey of academic writing tasks. *Written Communication, 1*(2), 247-280.

Britton, J., Burgess, T., Martin, N., McLeod, A., & Rosen, H. (1975). *The development of writing abilities (11-18)*. NCTE.

Burdick, M. N. (2011). Teacher negotiation and embedded process: A study of high school writing assignments. *Journal of Teaching Writing, 26*(2), 21-44.

Clark, I. (2005). A genre approach to writing assignments. *Composition Forum, 14*(2). https://compositionforum.com/issue/14.2/clark-genre-writing.php

Eblen, C. (1983). Writing across-the-curriculum: A survey of a university faculty's views and classroom practices. *Research in the Teaching of English, 17*(4), 343-348.

Eodice, M., Geller, A. E., & Lerner, N. (2016). *The meaningful writing project: Learning, teaching and writing in higher education*. University Press of Colorado.

Eodice, M., Geller, A. E., & Lerner, N. (2019). The power of personal connection for undergraduate student writers. *Research in the Teaching of English, 53*(4), 320-339.

Fink, S. B. (2012). The many purposes of course syllabi: Which are essential and useful? *Syllabus, 1*(1), 1–12.

Gardner, T. (2008). *Designing writing assignments*. NCTE. https://wac.colostate.edu/books/gardner/

Gere, A., Swofford, S., Silver, N., & Pugh, M. (2015). Interrogating disciplines/disciplinarity in WAC/WID: An institutional study. *College Composition and Communication, 67*(2), 243-266.

Harris, M. (2010). Assignments from hell: The view from the writing center. In P. Sullivan, H. Tinberg, & S. Blau (Eds.), *What is "college level" writing, volume 2: Assignments, readings, and student writing samples* (pp. 183-206). NCTE.

Horner, B. (2000). *Terms of work for composition: A materialist critique*. SUNY Press.

Horner, B. (2016). *Rewriting composition: Terms of exchange*. Southern Illinois University Press.

Hyon, S. (2008). Convention and inventiveness in an occluded academic genre: A case study of retention–promotion–tenure reports. *English for Specific Purposes, 27*(2), 175-192.

LaFrance, M. & Polk, T. (2018). *A report on the constraints that impact instruction in writing intensive courses*. George Mason University. https://wac.gmu.edu/wp-content/uploads/Constraints-Impacting-WI-Instruction.pdf.

Melzer, D. (2003). Assignments across the curriculum: A survey of college writing. *Language and Learning across the Disciplines, 6*(1), 86-110.

Melzer, D. (2009). Writing assignments across the curriculum: A national study of college writing. *College Composition and Communication, 61*(2), 240-261.

Melzer, D. (2014). *Assignments across the curriculum: A national study of college writing*. University Press of Colorado.

Neaderhiser, S. (2016). Hidden in plain sight: Metaphors of composition in teaching statements. *Composition Forum, 33*, 14 pp. https://compositionforum.com/issue/33/hidden.php.

Scott, T. (2009). *Dangerous writing: Understanding the political economy of composition*. Utah State University Press

Swales, J. M. (1996). Occluded genres in the academy: The case of the submission letter. In E. Ventola & A. Mauranen (Eds.), *Academic writing: Intercultural and textual issues* (pp. 45–58). John Benjamins.

Thaiss, C., & Zawacki, T. M. (2006). *Engaged writers and dynamic disciplines: Research on the academic writing life*. Boynton/Cook.

Review

AMY CICCHINO

Dannels, Deanna P., Patricia R. Palmerton, and Amy L. H. Gaffney. *Oral Communication in the Disciplines: A Resource for Teacher Development and Training.* Parlor Press, 2017. ($32; 252 pp., paperback)

WAC scholars have long argued that writing pedagogy serves students in two ways. First, through engaging with writing, students can more deeply learn the content knowledge of a discipline or field (e.g., Emig, 1977; Mayher, Lester, and Pradl, 1983; Applebee, 1985). Second, in considering writing as a situated practice, students can begin asking how the communities they belong to (or wish to enter) write (e.g., Russell, 1997; Thaiss and Zawacki, 2006; Deane and O'Neill, 2011).

CAC scholars further broadened WAC's mission to include a wider range of communicative forms, including writing in addition to oral, visual, and electronic forms of communication (Reiss, Selfe, and Young, 1998; Dannels, 2001; Duffelmeyer and Elletson, 2005; Vrchota and Russell, 2013). Building on this research, in *Oral Communication in the Disciplines: A Resource for Teacher Development and Training*, Deanna P. Dannels, Patricia R. Palmerton, and Amy L. Housley Gaffney take up oral communication in the non-communication course, arguing that oral communication literacy is exigent in higher education and a valuable facet in the professional preparation of students across disciplines. Informed by their expansive expertise in communication, administration, and rhetoric, they offer instructors a clear blueprint to the development of oral communication activities and assignments situated in existing content goals and disciplinary communities.

Throughout the book, the authors model a clear approach to curricular design that expands faculty knowledge of oral communication in addition to a general understanding of integrated course design. Accompanying this approach is a robust collection of examples from across the disciplines. The easy-to-follow frame for assignment design (described in further detail below) illustrates that this book could be picked up by instructors with little knowledge of communication and varying levels of teaching experience to create meaningful oral communication activities and assignments in their courses. In all, this book offers instructors commonsense but theoretically informed approaches and detailed assignment examples for integrating oral communication in their courses. In devoting an entire book to deeply focusing on oral communication pedagogy, the authors argue that student success in and beyond college is supported by one's ability to effectively communicate orally.

Dannels, Palmerton, and Gaffney take a contextualized, rhetorical approach to oral communication literacy within the disciplines, asking readers to reflect on "what counts as a competent communicator in [their] course or discipline?" (p. 11). The book is written to serve an audience outside of communications and is pragmatic and pedagogical (as its title implies). Chapter one explains concepts like writing-to-learn; communication-to-learn; communication literacy; and goals-based, discipline-specific curriculum development. The authors argue that integrating oral communication alongside learning processes can lead to deeper engagement and comprehension for students, that industry partners identify a lack of oral literacy in new employees and value oral ability generally, and that oral literacy can foster more universal abilities like engaged citizenship (p. 6–9). Chapter two introduces the framing for the rest of the book, which is meant to walk the reader—perhaps an instructor hesitant about integrating oral communication in their course—through the act of designing, delivering, and assessing communications activities that forward the existing outcomes in their courses. The authors outline a five-part frame that includes considering local and disciplinary contexts, identifying course outcomes and asking how oral communication might encourage these outcomes, designing informal activities and more formal assignments that support oral literacy, supporting students and anticipating challenges related to oral communication tasks, and responding to and assessing oral communication in a disciplinary context outside of communications.

In designing curricula, Dannels, Palmerton, and Gaffney employ a model that looks much like integrated course design (Fink, 2003), and, therefore, begins by asking readers to consider their local and disciplinary contexts as well as the outcomes for their particular courses. While these chapters align oral communication literacy to institutional goals, they also speak to hesitancies instructors might have towards oral communication in the classroom such as a lack of class time, instructor labor, a fear of not having communication expertise, class size, and a question about whether oral communication will be just another passing fad in institutional initiatives (p. 28–33). For WAC administrators, these hesitancies most likely stir feelings of déjà vu paralleling the many reasons instructors in the disciplines are reluctant to integrate writing activities in their courses. Responding to these hesitancies, the authors, then, explain the benefits of oral communications integration, such as its promotion of critical thinking, problem solving, and student-centered pedagogy as well as its role in disciplinary professionalization. However, they assert several times throughout the text that "[i]f particular activities or assignments do not help" with "achiev[ing] your course goals and outcomes [. . .] don't use them" (p. 37). By showing how oral communication can integrate with content and learning goals, the authors break down assumptions that disciplinary faculty often carry about WAC/WID/CAC programs: that communication development will be yet another thing they have to do in classes on top of content instruction. Instead, the authors refocus readers on how oral communication can further existing learning goals.

Chapters four and five walk the reader through informal activity and formal assignment design. The design process has seven steps:

1. Delineate learning outcomes and forms of inquiry
2. Identify the structure of the task you want students to complete
3. Articulate the particular areas of content you want students to focus on
4. Design prompts/tasks that have multiple possible responses and audiences
5. Designate guidelines for interaction and potential relational issues
6. Set clear expectations for outcomes of the exercise and, if appropriate, instructions for reporting the results of the process/product
7. Hold students accountable for their communication choices and behaviors in these activities. (p. 47)

Then, the authors break down each of the steps, offering examples of oral communication assignments in development through each stage. These examples are particularly helpful to instructors interested in beginning to integrate oral communication in their courses but unsure of where to begin or instructors looking to freshen up existing activities and assignments. They range in disciplinary and course contexts, offering readers a glimpse into what is possible.

Chapters six through ten explain the assistance students might need in completing oral communication tasks. The authors begin by tackling the common fears or apprehensions students might have related to speaking in public settings—even through informal speaking activities—as well as some strategies for managing this apprehension empathetically. Chapters seven and eight deeply focus on the two most common communication tasks: class discussion and group work. For instructors already using discussion and group work, these chapters explain how scaffolding and explicit expectations can yield more engaging experiences for students and instructors. They begin by stating that expectations for these tasks "vary dramatically" from one course to the next; therefore, a students' previous experiences with class discussion or group work might conflict with "what we expect [...] in our own classes" (121). Students' social and cultural norms, they state, can similarly shape students' oral communication in the classroom.[1] In supporting students' various points of entry, the authors suggest instructors take the same rhetorical, situated approach with clearly identified expectations at the beginning of a communication task and deliberate scaffolding throughout that task. Chapter nine gives instructors strategies for dealing with common, yet difficult, class situations related to oral communication tasks: aggression or disrespect in classroom discussion, group conflicts, and vulnerable moments that can arise when students are interacting with individuals who have different ideas, beliefs, and behaviors than themselves. In moments where instructors might be rendered speechless or unsure of how to respond, the authors offer valuable starting points for response.

The final section tackles evaluation: this section is helpful for thinking more critically about how assessment tools can be developed in alignment with outcomes. It begins by encouraging instructors to focus only on the aspects of oral communication that are directly related to an assignment's learning goals (p. 175). Just as with the chapters on assignment design, the authors provide a range of example evaluations; however, they largely rely on rubrics and scoring guides as the tools for evaluating student work. The authors, furthermore, detail how to frame feedback to reach students using Feedback Intervention Theory, which focuses on "meta-task features," "the learning of the tasks," and "reducing the feedback standard gap" while respecting students' desires to "act independently" (214). The strategies given here can easily move into written and visual forms of evaluation, giving instructors more knowledge of feedback and response strategies writ large.

In evaluating this book, my greatest critique is that in crafting a straightforward book that is readable for a general audience, the authors gloss over what are sometimes messy and complicated aspects to curricular design and assessment. This is most clearly seen in the assessment section, which flattens assessment to focus heavily on a particular assessment tool, rubrics. In a book that gives instructors so much agency in choosing and designing assignments, a more comprehensive range of assessment options would have been a nice addition. Instead of situating a rubric as one of many possible tools for assessment, in their description of the process of developing an assessment tool, the authors label this step simply as "create rubrics" (174). An entire chapter subsequently follows explaining how to choose which type of rubric might match an instructor's assignment design. From an authorial perspective, this might be a streamlined choice: instructors will want to know how to assess their students' oral communication tasks; rubrics will get the job done and are widely

---

1. It is important to note that the authors do not take up students' disabilities that impact oral instruction in these pages.

accepted. However, assessment scholars in writing studies have shown rubrics to be problematic in that they misrepresent the assessment process as easily definable and can lead to more rigid interpretations of what success on an assignment looks like (Wilson, 2006; Kohn, 2006; Inoue, 2015; Cirio, 2019). In the context of this text, rubrics are largely presented as the main option for assessing oral communication tasks and are never questioned or problematized.

This single concern is offset by the largely good work being done by Dannels, Palmerton, and Gaffney in this book. For faculty interested in expanding the oral communication offerings in their courses, this text can take them from conceptualization to delivery and assessment with approachable frameworks and multiple examples. For administrators who want to offer faculty a straightforward resource or introduce oral communication tasks into the contexts of a professional development program (such as a reading group or workshop), *Oral Communication in the Disciplines: A Resource for Teacher Development and Training* is a valuable resource. Besides being helpful and straightforward, it articulates the importance of oral communication in the professionalization and preparation of students across the disciplines. If WAC programs want to prepare students to be effective communicators, they must be forwarding all forms of communication, including oral communication.

References

Applebee, A. N. (1985). Writing and reasoning. *Review of Educational Research, 54*(4), 577–96.

Cirio, J. (2019). Meeting the promise of negotiations: Situating negotiated rubrics with students' prior experiences. *WPA: Writing Program Administration, 42*(2), 100–18.

Dannels, D. (2001). Time to speak up: A theoretical framework for situated pedagogy and practice for communication across the curriculum. *Communication Education, 50*(2), 14458.

Deane, M., & P. O'Neill. (2011). *Writing in the disciplines.* New York, NY: Palgrave MacMillan.

Duffelmeyer, B., & A. Ellertson. (2005). Critical visual literacy: Multimodal communication across the curriculum. *Across the Disciplines, 2.* Retrieved from https://wac.colostate.edu/atd/visual/dufflemeyer_ellerston.cfm

Emig, J. (1977). Writing as a mode of learning. *College Composition and Communication,* 28, 122–28.

Fink, D. L. (2003). *Creating significant learning experiences: An integrated approach to designing college courses.* San Francisco, CA: Jossey-Bass.

Inoue, A. B. (2015). *Antiracist writing assessment ecologies: Teaching and assessing writing for a socially just future.* Fort Collins, CO and Anderson, SC: WAC Clearinghouse and Parlor Press.

Kohn, A. (2006). The trouble with rubrics. *English Journal, 95*(4), 12–15.

Mayher, J., Lester, N., & Pradl. G. M. (1983). *Learning to write: Writing to learn.* Monclair, NJ: Boynton/Cook Publishers.

Reiss, D., Selfe, D., & Young, A. (1998). *Electronic communication across the curriculum.* Urbana, IL: National Council of Teachers of English.

Russell, D. (1997). Writing to learn to do: WAC, WAW, WAW—wow. *Language and Learning across the Disciplines, 2*(2), 3–8.

Thaiss, C., & Zawacki, T. M. (2006). *Engaged writers and dynamic disciplines: Research on the academic writing life.* Portsmouth, NH: Boynton.

Vrchota, D. A., & Russell, D. R. (2013). WAC/WID meets CXC/CID: A dialog between writing studies and communication studies. *The WAC Journal, 24,* 49–61.

Wilson, M. (2006). *Rethinking rubrics in writing assessment.* Portsmouth, NH: Heinemann.

Contributors

Linda Adler-Kassner is Professor of Writing, Faculty Director of the Center for Innovative Teaching, Research, and Learning, and Associate Dean of Undergraduate Education at UC Santa Barbara. She is author, coauthor, or coeditor of eleven books and many articles and chapters. These include *Naming What We Know: Threshold Concepts of Writing Studies* (2015) and *ReConsidering What We Know: Learning Thresholds in Writing, Composition, Rhetoric, and Literacy* (University Press of Colorado/Utah State UP 2019). Former chair of the Conference on College Composition and Communication and former president of the Council of Writing Program administrators, her research and teaching focuses on working with faculty on epistemologically inclusive teaching.

Jon M. Balzotti is an assistant professor in the English department at Brigham Young University, Provo, Utah, where he teaches courses in technical writing, proposal writing, and style. His research interests include professional communication pedagogy, workplace genres, and digital learning environments.

Amy Cicchino is Associate Director for the Office of University Writing at Auburn University. Cicchino specializes in writing program administration, digital multimodality, and writing in the disciplines. Her work has appeared in *WPA: Writing Program Administration, Research in Online Literacy Education (ROLE)*, and *ePortfolio as Curriculum* (2019).

Brad Peters is Professor of English at Northern Illinois University. He has coordinated writing across the curriculum for twenty-one years, founded the University Writing Center, and has served in several administrative capacities: UWC director, director of first-year composition, undergraduate studies director, and acting chair of English. He co-edited the *Journal of the Assembly for Expanded Perspectives on Learning* with Joonna Smitherman Trapp for eight years. Publication interests include writing program administration, writing pedagogy, and medieval rhetoric.

Amy D. Williams is an assistant professor of English at Brigham Young University, Provo, Utah. She teaches courses in composition theory and pedagogy, professional writing, and style. She researches writing pedagogy and is especially interested in how students experience writing in and outside of classrooms.

the WAC Journal

SUBSCRIPTIONS

The WAC Journal is an open-access, blind, peer-viewed journal published annually by Clemson University, Parlor Press and the WAC Clearinghouse. It is published annually in print by Parlor Press and Clemson University. Digital copies of the journal are simultaneously published at The WAC Clearinghouse in PDF format for free download, http://wac.colostate.edu/journal/. Print subscriptions support the ongoing publication of the journal and make it possible to offer digital copies as open access.

- One year: $25
- Three years: $65
- Five years: $95

You can subscribe to *The WAC Journal* and pay securely by credit card or PayPal online at http://www.parlorpress.com/wacjournal. Or you can send your name, email address, and mailing address along with a check (payable to Parlor Press) to

Parlor Press
3015 Brackenberry Drive
Anderson SC 29621

Subcribe to the
WAC Journal

Clemson University   WAC Clearinghouse

PARLOR PRESS
EQUIPMENT FOR LIVING

New, in Living Color!

Exquisite Corpse: Studio Art-Based Writing Practices in the Academy ed. by Kate Hanzalik and Nathalie Virgintino

The Afterlife of Discarded Objects: Memory and Forgetting in a Culture of Waste by Andrei Guruianu and Natalia Andrievskikh

Type Matters: The Rhetoricity of Letterforms ed. Christopher Scott Wyatt and Dànielle Nicole DeVoss (**BEST DESIGN AWARD-Ingram**)

New Releases

Creole Composition: Academic Writing and Rhetoric in the Anglophone Caribbean edited by Vivette Milson-Whyte, Raymond Oenbring, and Brianne Jaquette

Retellings: Opportunities for Feminist Research in Rhetoric and Composition Studies edited by Jessica Enoch and Jordynn Jack

Tracing Invisible Lines: An Experiment in Mystoriography by David Prescott-Steed

KONSULT: Theopraxesis by Gregory L. Ulmer

Best of the Journals in Rhetoric and Composition 2018

Other People's English: Code-Meshing, Code-Switching, and African American Literacy by Vershawn Ashanti Young, et al.

Congratulations, Award Winners!

Strategies for Writing Center Research by Jackie Grutsch McKinnie. **Best Book Award, International Writing Centers Association (2017)**

Antiracist Writing Assessment Ecologies: Teaching and Assessing Writing for a Socially Just Future by Asao Inoue, **Best Book Award, CCCC, Best Book, Council of Writing Program Administrators (2017)**

The WPA Outcomes Statement—A Decade Later edited by Nicholas N. Behm, Gregory R. Glau, Deborah H. Holdstein, Duane Roen, & Edward M. White, **Best Book Award, Council of Writing Program Adminstrators (2015)**

www.parlorpress.com

www.ingramcontent.com/pod-product-compliance
Lightning Source LLC
Chambersburg PA
CBHW030119170426
43198CB00009B/675